Twayne's United States Authors Series

Sylvia E. Bowman, *Editor*
INDIANA UNIVERSITY

Robert Herrick

ROBERT HERRICK

by Louis J. Budd

Duke University

 178

Twayne Publishers, Inc. :: New York

FOR CATHY AND DAVID

Preface

The literary career of Robert Herrick was, all in all, a string of surprises, and not always happy ones. At times, he seemed to change direction with every novel he published, thereby bewildering the admirers of the one before it. Just as *Together*, his most ambitious work, was rushed into a sixth printing, he complained to Hamlin Garland: "There is a good deal in the book that I wish were better. But there is always the next time! Though I shan't do another 'realistic novel' for a long, long day—something better than that I hope, to take the taste out of my mouth."[1] Now, looking back over his career, few admirers can take any comfort in his resulting turn into the strained allegory of *A Life for a Life*, in his uninspired returns to the short story, or in his frenetic propaganda during the early days of World War I. Yet the broad look backward does show that he steadily refined both his sensibility and his art, seldom regressing for long, and that he kept acquiring fresh perspectives on human character and fictional technique, even though he never caught up with the avant-gardes that proliferated during his lifetime. While indifferent to experimenting for its own sake, he continually outgrew his attitudes, long after most minds begin repeating themselves.

This growth does not mean Herrick finally became a major figure, unrecognized because his public had lost interest. Overstatement will not help his case or the critical objective. He was more nearly a minor writer, we can agree—so long as we remain aware that truly major writers are scarce by definition, that a "star" system currently distorts not merely the movie and television world, and that minor writers can add valuable insights. The case for Herrick need not depend primarily on his "transitional" qualities nor on the more respectable point that he is worthwhile as a social historian. He wrote some solidly good novels: *The Web of Life*, *The Memoirs of an American Citizen*, *One Woman's Life*, *Homely Lilla*, and *The End of Desire*. (Happily, these titles run in an advancing order not only chronologically but also, pretty much, esthetically.) With *Chimes* he came as close as anybody to a perceptive and authentic novel of campus life, a subject that has evaded completely satisfying treatment for perhaps insurmountable reasons. *Sometime* ended his career with a utopian romance too hopeful for our age of myopic disillusion, which prefers the anti-utopia driven by bitterness; his earthly paradise also had more intelligent counts against it, but it still is worth picking up out of the heaps of old and new books. In short, our literature is not so rich nor are we so rightfully busy with grander matters that even the best of his fiction should be ignored.

It certainly was not, either here or abroad, during his most successful years. In 1908 an American magazine ran a translation of an admiring essay on his work that took three installments in a leading Danish organ of criticism.[2] Young or old, Herrick aimed high with no conscious relenting toward the appetite for entertainment. After judging his contemporaries harshly, he summed up: "I feel that American novelists are afraid of being dull, and have the irritating American defect of not taking themselves seriously enough."[3] His fiction solemnly assessed American life from the 1890's to the 1930's, keeping pace with events and intellectual crises. Fortunately, he started without the blinders of the small-town myth, being forced to decide in his boyhood that pride in class and the lust for status were as strong on Main Street as anywhere else; in *The Web of Life*, escape to the village is declined as a solution for rebels against the corrupting city; and, with no cause for future regrets, Van Harrington, his best-known capitalist, flees from the petty stagnation of an Indiana town. With his very first novel Herrick focused on upper-middle-class life in a metropolis, grasping before Dreiser the potency of the city and insisting on class patterns in spite of a consensus that they applied only when self-inflicted in the lower depths. From the outset, he was ready to write the novel of manners, a genre closed to most minds of our leveling republic.

Yet at his keenest he went deeper than the surfaces of the plush drawing rooms, broke through the illusion of comfortable status. He was alert to a new kind of woman—triumphantly married, untyrannized, restless, rootless, socially ambitious, unfulfilled by her shrinking duties—who sprang up in large enough numbers to make a fascinating and exasperating subclass. He was also quick to see the new professional men—architects, university teachers, physicians—grappling with their problems of integrity, particularly those posed by a business society and its pressures of moneymaking, corporate values, machined standards, and conspicuous consumption. His stance toward the tycoon's world became radical rather than liberal or—what looked more logical politically at the time—Progressive; though at first hazy about economics, he really did not hope for a softening of the ways and ends of capitalism but for some high-minded revelation. An astute foreign critic concluded in 1936 that Herrick was the "last important representative of American democracy in literature."[4] This judgment, easily mistaken as trite or empty, meant soundly that he had always subscribed to natural rights and to a society oriented toward inner freedom rather than toward property and that he was still hoping, as tenaciously as Thomas Paine, for a new man in a New World.

He differed crucially from a Paine in that his moral energy turned inward irresistibly. Bred as one of the last Puritans, he would test everything by his conscience, by a personal scale of right and wrong; the content of his scale changed but not the terms nor the compulsion to apply them. Very early he suspected that moral values were increasingly weak for most Americans, and—decades ahead of what would harden into a cliché—sent his characters in search of sound moorings instead of reliance on shifting and impersonal institutions. Like Henry James, another puritan who gave off a deceiving air of urbanity, he seldom mentioned God but brooded about ethical choice. In fact, with Herrick the question of integrity in a money-getting, status-hungry world holds the forefront for the first time in our fiction; William Dean Howells' useful warnings seem evasive by contrast. Like a relentless preacher to the Massachusetts Bay Colony, Herrick fought men's instinct to explain away their lapses of principle, and he again and again trained his sights on the illusions—love, success, freedom—by which men hid the failures of the inner self or of the outward world that it had created. This attack on illusions would, through a welter of other drives, make and keep Herrick a proponent of Realism and an important force in its full development.

This importance has been underestimated, partly because of the accelerated pace of our literature. Within a few years after Howells reached his own peak with *A Hazard of New Fortunes* (1890), Herrick had gone a long step beyond it both in objectivity of method and in toughness of mind. But Stephen Crane, wonderfully precocious, had already leaped past any other advances to be made before the 1920's. Likewise, though *The Web of Life*, Herrick's first major novel, was clearly superior in some ways to *Sister Carrie*, which appeared in the same year, Dreiser's meat-ax Naturalism made Herrick's rapier-like Realism seem genteel, at times even to himself. In 1935, for a lecture at the University of Puerto Rico, he split American literature into two traditions: the derivative, with which he humbly grouped himself; and the native, exemplified by Mark Twain, Whitman, Finley Peter Dunne, and Dreiser. The inclusiveness of this second group betrays a more crucial weakness, not in Herrick but in his inheritance.

Beginning to publish during the reign of genteel evasiveness, Herrick never felt securely backed by either forebears or allies. He would have profited immensely from finding a mature, aggressively Realistic tradition here like the famous one in France that did inspire most of his literary courage. At least he helped to build such a tradition on native grounds, and Grant C. Knight declares that he "had an effect upon American history which cannot yet be fully calculated."[5] But he was not a literary statesman or politician; he avoided coteries, to the detriment of his reputation if nothing else, because he lost out on many of those strategically placed review articles that would have kept it fresh and growing. More vitally, he was not quite talented or fiery enough to arouse a following, especially since our rebels typically thought they were beginning all over again and were in no mood to copy anyone knowingly.

Still, Herrick's achievement rises above the ever widening torrent of books. Newton Arvin, in a summing up that he might later have regretted as too generous, credited Herrick with "three of the most impressive novels in our literature" and with the "most capacious and the most truly critical mind at work in American fiction since Howells and Norris."[6] Except as a mode of emphasis, comparative rating of authors is inhumane in both senses of the word. Furthermore, Herrick is best served if we treat his talent as more minor than major. Yet his is a complex, engaging, and thoughtful body of fiction worth knowing in detail.

The following chapters concentrate on this fiction, approaching it in the order he published it and resisting the temptation to wax ironic or hearty about his almost stealthily tempestuous life or to depersonalize him into an index of the subcultures that shaped him most. In other words, Herrick is taken here in the role he always came back to, after no matter what renunciations. Since his latest novel often was partly a reaction against the one before, it makes most sense when it is considered in the pattern of his fitful evolution. He also worked and thought in larger cycles, which handily shape my divisions into chapters. Above all, since his artistic career was a restless, continual search, it is best understood in sequence. He saw all kinds of men as bound by the accumulating logic of their deeds, and we can see him most richly the same way.

LOUIS J. BUDD

Duke University

Acknowledgments

I am grateful especially to the wisely liberal policy of the Division of Archives and Manuscripts of the University of Chicago Library for allowing me full use of the Robert Herrick Papers. During my reading in them, Frank G. Burke, then the assistant curator, was extremely helpful. The staff of the Duke University Library has again helped me in many ways, and the Duke University Research Council has supported me with grants for expenses and a faculty summer research fellowship. Professor Blake Nevius of the University of California at Los Angeles has volunteered encouragement and information in what I like to think of as the true spirit of academic learning.

Contents

Chronology

1868   Robert Herrick born April 26 in Cambridge, Massachusetts, where he grew up; spent summers in Boxford, Massachusetts.

1881   Entered Cambridge High School.

1885   Entered Harvard University with slender means.

1887   Left in February on nine months' tour of the Caribbean area, Mexico, and the American Far West; published his first story in Harvard *Advocate*.

1888   In May, his first story appeared in Harvard *Monthly*, of which he soon became editor.

1890   Graduated from Harvard; became instructor in English at the Massachusetts Institute of Technology.

1892   Spent summer in Europe; in winter began work on first, incomplete novel, which dealt with academic life.

1893   Moved to newly founded University of Chicago as an instructor in rhetoric; first story accepted by *Scribner's Magazine*.

1894   Married his first cousin, Harriet Peabody Emery; published a story in *Atlantic Monthly*.

1897   Published novelette *The Man Who Wins* and collected a second volume, *Literary Love-Letters and Other Stories*.

1898   Scored modest success with *The Gospel of Freedom*; collected another volume of short stories, *Love's Dilemmas*; first child died.

1899   Collaborated on successful and influential textbook, *Composition and Rhetoric for Schools*; son born.

1900   Achieved full maturity with *The Web of Life*, which aroused tempest in Chicago; second daughter born.

1901   Gave first major proof of his "idealistic" vein with *The Real World*; second daughter died.

1904   Scored critical success with *The Common Lot*.

1905   His most lasting novel, *The Memoirs of an American Citizen*, appeared in book form after being serialized.

1907   Reached a crisis, partly emotional, in his health; wrote "The Master of the Inn," a popular success.

1908   Won much notoriety, as well as sales, with his longest and most ambitious novel, *Together*.

1910   Reacted against recent notoriety with awkwardly allegorical *A Life for a Life*, a disappointment on all counts.

1911   The last of his idealistic novels, *The Healer*, found a shrinking public.

1912   Bought house and land in York Village, Maine.

1913   Tried his only potboiler, *His Great Adventure*; *One Woman's Life* brought gossip and final separation from his wife.

1914   *Clark's Field* partly revived his reputation though sales were disappointing.

1915   Traveled in Europe, from April to August, as commentator on war; wrote first major autobiographical piece, "Myself" (unpublished).

1916   Finally divorced from wife; traveled again to Europe; collected his newspaper dispatches in *The World Decision*.

1917   Returned in fall to teaching at University of Chicago; disenchanted over World War I.

1923   Resigned from professorship; began life of traveling and free-lance writing with base in Maine; *Homely Lilla* published.

1924   *Waste* summed up his life and ideas, in light of current politics.

1925   *Wanderings*, a book of four novellas, returned to less contentious note.

1926   *Chimes* summed up his judgments on university life.

1929   Lost heavily in the stock-market crash.

1931   Taught during winter term of Rollins College in Florida; *Little Black Dog* hurried into obscurity by publisher's bankruptcy; began series of unpublished autobiographical writings.

1932   Wintered in Mexico; *The End of Desire* capped his career as a novelist.

1933   *Sometime*, his utopian romance, showed surprising hopefulness.

1935   Appointed as government secretary of the Virgin Islands.

1938   Died on December 23 in Virgin Islands; buried in York Village, Maine.

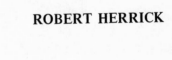

ROBERT HERRICK

CHAPTER 1

The Rise to Power

I *The Yankee Background*

Even without the Freudian insistence that personality must be traced back to the womb, Robert Herrick demands consideration of his childhood before we can begin to understand him as a novelist. From his first coherent emotion he seldom felt fully at home in this world. Looking back, near the end of his life he would recognize that his attitude toward outer experience had always blurred into a sense of dislocation, of missed rapport. He would more specifically see that in early adolescence he had acquired the habit of "creating for himself as a relief from his disagreeable environment an island of ideal peace, beauty, and serenity. . . . In various forms and under many different aspects this mood of another worldliness came upon him increasingly."[1] Many a novelist has followed this pattern, which obviously can lead toward creating a vicarious realm on the printed page. In Herrick's case, it led also to a fierce idealism that insisted on measuring the shortcomings of the loud world, too seldom with ironic wonder rather than disdain. But he was beguiled enough by this world or convinced of its vitality or impelled by his puritanism to subdue it that he would struggle to set it down accurately, with explicit or implicit guides for improving it.

The precise workings of his early retreat and rebellion are naturally hard to discover now. Any interpretation, Freudian or otherwise, suffers the weakness of having to depend too much on Herrick's formal testimony. Still, it was given sincerely, makes good sense, shows a strong core of similarity in its repeated versions over a span of about twenty-five years, and checks basically with the several uses of his boyhood in his novels. Furthermore, encouragingly, he gained deepening vision into his origins instead of clouding the truth with proliferating and defensive fantasies, like Mark Twain.

One of Herrick's last insights was obvious yet fundamental. He had, it turns out, always believed in what he labeled the American "tradition," or what has lately been styled the American "dream"; he believed in its unique and noble potentialities, even while recognizing that its catchwords were often used to gild low motives or mass vulgarity. During the acrid soul-searching of the Great Depression, he declared that for all of his "conscious life" he had trusted that his society—built on a "cultural base differing from that of all other peoples, due to the physical environment, racial inheritances, and historical development of the American people"— stressed to a new degree the "values of individuality, independence, self-assurance, adventurous experimentation."[2] In effect, he had trusted so well in this ideal that, along with private drives, it kept him from becoming a marginal man and especially from being an expatriate or esthete—the two roles of rejection likeliest for him. While resisting the snug doctrine that progress was both our birthright and soundest touchstone, he did subscribe to the other guiding tenets of later nineteenth-century America—political democracy, faith in moral law, reverence for individualism, and nebulous but fervent faith in the uplift of the fine arts.

Indeed, he felt he had, as a New Englander, a special duty as well as a stake in advancing this tradition. His native section was generally still accepted as the seedbed of the American dream, and he never seriously doubted that reading of history. Luckily for his writing career, however, his New England loyalties did not for long, if ever, tie him to the Brahmin worthies still active in and around Cambridge, Massachusetts, where Herrick was born and reared. Though he saw both Henry Wadsworth Longfellow and James Russell Lowell in the flesh, an aside in one of his early novels shunts Longfellow to the "imitative period of our arts." This complaint is surprising, for Herrick never showed an appetite for Whitman or other iconoclasts in poetry, never rebelled as directly as most writers do against the literary tradition in which they grew up. The vital rebellion was tacit: he never aspired to promulgate Victorian lyrics, closet dramas, or rhymed homiletics. He felt too much of a need to grapple with the daily workings of society.

Pressed on him directly, the Brahmin lack of respect for the novel, particularly as an evaluation of the teeming here and now, left nevertheless a lasting mark. Twice in his memoirs he recalled letting his habitually sympathetic father know that he hoped to create fiction, only to be admonished gently to aim for "more serious" or "real" books that help "mental improvement." He described the rebuff with an air of having transcended it, but this was far from the emotional truth. He never embraced "art for art's sake," even in its vaguest form. His novels invariably gave food for sober thought, with side effects very much like moral as well as mental improvement. Spurning the primitive liberty of the slice-of-life school, he judged character as severely as many Puritan divines and ended if not on an uplifting, then a firmly hortatory note. He helps us understand why the Brahmins produced so few novels worth even skimming today and, indeed, so few novels.

The New England mind he otherwise saw so objectively that he might seem to have rejected most of it. In 1931, defending the dignity of a beloved dog of vague pedigree, he sneered at how many of the last Brahmins "had a distinctive homeliness, which was all that their pure race had bequeathed them." He also recalled sardonically that the son of Charles W. Eliot, one of Harvard's mightiest presidents, had felt unhappy, even bewildered during a short visit in Cuba because nobody knew of his father's eminence. Publicly, Herrick sighed in retrospect: "Superiority of inheritance, of education, of pronunciation, of manners, of morals, above all! The true New Englander was stamped by an inward satisfaction that often made him seem priggish, provincial, and odious. . . ."[3] This indictment, on the surface at least, fitted some fictional Yankees shaped after himself, though its mainspring was his sense of exclusion, of feeling classed as inferior because money had not countersigned his own pure pedigree. The unpublished "Mr. Maggot's Fortune," which cheerfully berates his plunge into the stock market during the 1920's, opens: "I was born of poor (and hence presumably honest) parents in that part of the U.S.A. where poverty if not a disgrace was an ignominy. . . ." Still, neither his friends nor his enemies ever doubted that he hailed from the heart of old-family Massachusetts.

In its main thrust "Mr. Maggot's Fortune" really protested the decline of the ideal Puritan attitude toward wealth, one sturdily held by every major hero in his novels. As recently as his youth in the Massachusetts of the 1870's—he later boasted—it was considered "ill bred to talk about money, either what one had or hadn't," to make display of any sort, to base self-respect on a bankbook, or even to "waste material things" on the "flesh." On too many counts he kept the Yankee sense of "superiority" that he flayed in others. Pridefully, his most careful venture in autobiography began by insisting that his "every drop of blood" was Puritan, that his "youth was nurtured completely in puritan influences." The record shows bountifully 'that he struck others as—his later sex life notably aside—the typically smug Harvardite. In spite of arguing that putting down roots was the important point, not the place where they went down, he stabilized what his biographer calls one of the "most peripatetic" lives of his generation by at last settling, blissfully and tenaciously, in York Village, Maine.

What ideal Puritanism meant to and for Herrick is clear; he never tired of spelling it out. Its restraint toward money sprang from a pervasive simplicity, a common-sense level of Henry Thoreau's austerity—a standard that Herrick never relaxed for his fictional characters, even while keeping his own affairs jumbled or heartily enjoying a touch of mink. Austerity he prized for its hair-shirt training in self-control but also for clearing the way toward purely intellectual ends. More basic than the arts or metaphysics, the intellectual life required the informed and disciplined mind. He criticized the business class much less for poor taste than for mental barrenness; and he naturally subscribed to great trust in education which helped make feasible his career as a university professor. His day-to-day groans about that career were private, breathed only to friends and dedicated allies on campus; though he inevitably came to feel that his own hours should be devoted to his fiction, he never denied the teachability of his fellow men. More vitally, never losing faith in the value of faith itself, he respected Puritanism for honoring the "need for religious expression" or some kind of "true religion," the self-confessed "master theme" of all his pages "as it must be in the lives of all serious persons."⁴ This navigating by idealism was not uniquely Puritan, of course, but the combination with other precepts was, especially when added to those spurring on his heroes, such as the need to subdue the world of fact to the world of ideal or the duty to tell the truth as one saw it.

Puritanism gave Herrick a positive center for his energies and values, a bulwark against the poundings of relativism, a synthesis for intellectual absolutism, rigor of action, and moral progress. It also focused his sense of dissent, of deploring the way that American society had headed and therefore of feeling charged to correct it. Most crucially of all, Puritanism taught him a "sense of responsibility of the duty of organized will," which proved its discipline by palpable and practical works while meeting the highest standards of integrity. This duty sparked his strongest drive but also his keenest torment, because he wanted the outward proofs of success without losing a spotless conscience. He at least recognized this dilemma as it torments others, observing that the characters of his novels before World War I were torn between success and conscience, often resenting unconsciously the "Be good or you will be punished" creed that kept them from enjoying fully the fruits of alluring materialism.

Now that advertising has sanctified "fun" as well as affluence, we soothingly forget how agonizing the choice was for a society also in love with moral absolutes. Usually too elevated to analyze his own market, Herrick granted that the "fact that I was always concerned with this spiritual drama in one form or another doubtless was the source of my appeal to serious readers, who felt in their own lives the divided call of their puritan ancestry and their modern world." (However, the assumption that such ancestry was common, despite the peak tide of immigrants, reduced the breadth of his appeal.)

II *Family Patterns*

In his private emotional economy, Puritanism hampered Herrick's "call" toward respecting his mother. On almost every count she violated or misused the New England tradition as he felt it, and she made a travesty of its summum bonum of integrity. Daughter of a fairly prominent Congregational minister, she took her brood to the Episcopalian church in Cambridge for reasons of status. (All of his career, most notably in *One Woman's Life* (1913), her son bristled at the notion of choosing a church on this basis.) Likewise, she served as his first, all-too-closely observed example of the gap between professed and practiced ethics and of the difference, which grated on Stephen Crane, between using "they" and "we" in bewailing sin. One of Herrick's undergraduate stories hit hard at the smugness of the conventionally pious and their reluctance to help the needy.

Symbolically, he remembered that he stopped prayers and churchgoing "as soon as" he got away to college. As a matter of fact, once compulsory chapel ended after his freshman year, he still attended often, rationalizing that he went to "hear some distinguished man and listen to the excellent music." Blaming his "sour dislike" on his mother, he did apparently quit churchgoing altogether when he moved to Chicago; but his religious sense—as a faith in the need for guiding principles—never wavered.

Mostly because of his mother, Herrick had such an unhappy childhood that his memories reached back little before the age of seven and were pathetically thin for a while after that. He had other deep causes for resenting her, especially her domineering misuse of her gentle, decently competent husband. As a result, Herrick's attitude toward women took painful courses—one that is much clearer in his private life where an ill-advised marriage soon brought prolonged bickering before a divorce and where he tardily but unflaggingly began a cavalier string of amours. Hindsight may find extreme patterns in his fiction but nothing pathological, no resentment so vindictive as Ernest Hemingway's. His fictional wives often exploit or dominate their husbands without the saving humor beneath which William Dean Howells, very happily mothered and wived, drew his more commonly henpecked husbands; yet Herrick's novels could tip the scales the opposite way. Unexpectedly, the broadest literary effect of his antipathy toward his mother was fortunate: it saved him from mariolatry, and his novels never sentimentalize woman in the nineteenth-century way that Mark Twain typified most glaringly. Naturally, they never subscribe therefore to the true Progressive's faith in family virtues as the cornerstone for the ideal society.

The subtleties of the tension between mother and son were complicated beyond our analysis today. But Herrick unquestionably writhed under her many-faced drive for status, which labored as hard on weekdays as Sundays. In his "First Memories" he declared, with accusatory detail, that the "germ of class distinction was insidiously instilled into the boy's mind." To be sure, his mother sprang from old stock, and Herrick could "doubt if a single one of my ancestors came to this country later than the middle of the seventeenth century"; furthermore, she claimed ties with some of the more successful families in the Bay Colony days, including the Hathornes. Unhappily, her delight in her patrician blood only made her jangle the children with her spleen over lost glories while embarrassing them with her devices for living beyond lower-middle-class means. Such are the paradoxes of human nature that her disapproving son overspent his ampler means much of his life. But his novels are hard on spendthrifts, particularly wives who spur husbands to earn more and more at the expense of inner peace and the true family welfare.

It would be logical emotionally if the son despised a father bullied by such a wife. Yet the son mainly felt pity for a victim whose meekness verged on the saintly. After all, the Herrick line also went far back; and the original Herrick in the New World had for an uncle the British poet, whose name the novelist bore. (He once smilingly obliged a young lady eager for the autograph of her favorite poet.) Seemingly on the rise, the novelist's father earned a degree from Dartmouth College and became a lawyer with a local fame for his legal publications and with enough income for modest respectability. Perhaps more out of love than fact, the son admired him as a high-minded casualty of refusing to go along with the times, to give up his scholarly leanings and turn into a salesman of legal tricks for the highest bidder. None of Herrick's many characters who opt for professional integrity over a plush income is derided as a weak-kneed dreamer.

Besides the lesson of integrity, his father's line supplied a summer home and emotional retreat at Boxford, Massachusetts, only thirteen miles from where the first farming Herrick had settled in 1638. Everyone, except perhaps the mother, hungrily welcomed this escape from a drab house in a drab section of Cambridge. While never fancying himself a Huckleberry Finn, the boy found healing pleasure in the countryside; unconvincingly somehow, most of his characters turned to simple nature for comfort and even inspiration at their inevitable crisis in ethics. During these summers Herrick spent much time around the home of his father's brother, still a farmer and a very successful one as well as truly head of a close-knit, placid, open-hearted family. This family must have reassured the nephew that the paternal line had not petered out or lost its touch for a practical success that dovetailed with moral serenity. More broadly, the plain household helped to check his bookish fastidiousness and to create the possibility of respect for folk smelling of hard work in the fields or bare-boarded kitchen. Even so, this respect grew dimmer than it should have been.

III *College Days*

Warmth for his mother's family rebounded a bit when the time came to think of college. His father's last tired gasp having left the widow with six children and no negotiable assets, Herrick seemed doomed to a clerk's stool until a cousin—George Herbert Palmer, a pillar of Harvard's department of philosophy—ruled that Herrick had ability deserving more education. So his maternal grandmother supplied the money with the understanding that he would emerge as the breadwinner for his mother and two sisters. Rescued more melodramatically than a Realistic novel could dare to allow, Herrick entered Harvard in the fall of 1885 with trembling and uncertainty. Later he claimed to have at this point first plumbed to the limit his social inferiority, which bred a lifelong discomfort of "not belonging." Surely this memory overstates both his inner turmoil and the outward signs of his low standing, even if he was as cowed as some sophomores intended.

His taut caution struck the restless extroverts as poise. None of his contemporaries at Harvard has recorded an impression of a timid, apologetic Herrick. By the time he had fleeting status as an upperclassman, Robert Morss Lovett—who was refreshingly staunch in self-respect—thought him a "youth of truly classical figure and beauty, and of an icy manner which he obviously tried to thaw." He already had that air of stiff-necked reserve which would soon awe his students, but he confessed later to eyeing the desirable girls around Cambridge "secretly but intensively." Probably the most revealing of his literary work at Harvard is a translation of Guy de Maupassant's "Isolation" (rendered by some as "Solitude"), a febrile monologue by a Parisian who warns that lovers never escape the prison of self, that all perceptive humans find true communication blocked, and that they learn to hide stoically their innermost soul. The translator undoubtedly felt, with masochistic twinges, that his hauteur covered a tempest of longing unsuspected by the dull world.

Yet, then or later, Herrick never thought of rejecting the Harvard spirit. Its current Brahmin version, which professed to engross the marrow of the Puritan heritage, suited him mentally and emotionally. He grimly enjoyed the shabby dormitories and the other buildings relatively encrusted with age in a raw New World. Prideful at having joined the main artery of the tradition that counted most here, he particularly valued Harvard's "scorn" of frivolous beauties, its "clean correctness and integrity of life," its devotion to the soul as well as the intellect, and its insistence on work performed rather than on gusty manifestos. Above all, in looking back a few years afterward, Herrick valued its "aristocratic bearing," meaning primarily "that intolerant love for the most excellent and but one excellence."[5] While not a distinguished student, he took his classes seriously. If he cut any capers, they have eluded memory; as a senior, he must have cast down, deliberately if need be, more than his share of burbling newcomers.

Fortunately for Herrick, the winds of change were blowing harder through Harvard's elms than he knew. As incidental touches show in an unpublished novel he soon wrote about the "Yard," a genuinely Bohemian circle had sprung up and, partly separate from it, a literary avant-garde. Even the mainstream, lately roiled by the elective system, had its cosmopolitan sources, whether of the older kind emanating from Charles E. Norton, the sniffish but learned champion of the fine arts, or the fresh mordancy encouraged by George Santayana, who eventually needed a wider arena. The undergraduate body had its full share of venturesome minds—Lovett, Bernard Berenson, the Hapgood brothers, William Vaughn Moody—ready to interpret sweepingly and contemporaneously their duty to know the best that had been thought and said in the world. Ironically, Herrick's horizons lifted also because of the kindness of Philip Abbot, a roommate who achieved the Puritan virtues "more nearly than any one I ever knew."

Herrick, invited to keep the wealthy Abbot company, broke out of his sophomore year and provincial limits to wander through the Caribbean, Mexico, California, Alaska, and the Southwest. Understandably, the trip brought "revelation" in myriad ways: he learned kinetically of the "sensuous beauty" teeming in warmer climates and the "bigness of things, of the world, of its variety." He also expanded his grasp of "human social complexity" by chumming on shipboard with a Roman Catholic priest who tried no black magic, by chatting with seedy adventurers who seemed more pathetic than criminal, or by mixing with coolly sinful stalwarts from the Senate of the United States who treated their official mission with thick-skinned cynicism. But Herrick's reactions ran mainly to wonder, delight, and, later, surprise because "all this stimulating of the senses did not make a romancer of me." The implication that gusto for color and amoral verve is foreign to Realism boded ill for his fiction. It at least proved again how deep were the Puritan roots of his mind and, furthermore, how much credit he gave them. His unpublished "Myself" ended comment on his great tour by exulting that "my puritan sense of purpose and fact kept me to the literary lines of realism in which my Harvard education confirmed me."

IV *Earliest Writing and Literary Creed*

Herrick wronged his literary principles in linking them so simply with orthodox patterns, though Puritanism could certainly foster a resolve to lay the truth bare. Postbellum Realism, especially if it did not invoke Emerson's praise of the "familiar and the low," often sprang from the widening gap between the official culture and the "great barbecue" that was becoming more brutal daily—a gap that his trip made clearer. Likewise, he wronged the Harvard of his youth in implying that it confirmed only one literary pattern, one grounded in austerity and moralism. Evolution-minded science and philosophical naturalism, once the intellectuals' resistance to Darwin collapsed, had swept through the Yard, stimulating a sterner look at the data of current life.

Even among those uninterested in science, European writers reflecting its latest shock waves were being read and debated. Herrick had quickly fastened on some of the most controversial figures, including Henrik Ibsen, one of whose plays he bravely reprinted in the Harvard *Monthly* during his editorship. In 1894, Frank Norris already an alumnus of San Francisco and Paris, gravitated to Harvard; though chilled by the same human climate Herrick found so congenial, Norris felt comfortable enough to begin his two most Naturalistic novels. By 1900 Harvard was almost notorious as a rallying place for rebels in belles lettres. On the practical level, Herrick profited also from the rising interest and liberality in the teaching of composition, which Barrett Wendell gradually made his personal empire.

In 1914, while conducting a sprightly column for the Chicago *Tribune*, Herrick reminisced that, because his father had shown such disdain toward novelists, he kept his "purpose hidden for a good many years." The less heart-tugging truth is that he wrote fiction doggedly from his freshman year onward and, without luck, soon tried to sell it to the big magazines. By March, 1887—before he was nineteen—he could preen over the first of several short stories in the Harvard *Advocate*; and he quickly moved into the pages of the new, more literary-minded Harvard *Monthly*, making his mark there in time to enjoy his term as editor. However, he had no intentions of becoming a midwife nor any visible fears that he could do no better than edit more talented minds.

As with all his fiction, his output at Harvard arouses more interest for its content than its manner—a useful distinction in spite of eloquent arguments that the two are organically inseparable for the arts. He patently began with no restiveness under conventional notions of form or technique. Rather, surprisingly severe toward his phase of adolescent fantasy, his early stories harped on the need to come to grips with reality. They were other-worldly, nevertheless, in showing no awareness for the socio-economic web in which we move. Their heroes hold to a path of self-inventory that implies a renunciation of vast horizons; indeed, one of his stories ("Disjecta Membra") for the Harvard *Monthly* explicitly preached that "A narrow range of life was all that the individual could hope to fill."[6] In his only major resemblance to his meteoric contemporary, Stephen Crane, Herrick clearly felt that a man had best take as his highest responsibility the honesty of his vision about himself. Crane too, we tend to forget, had absorbed a sternly Protestant training before pressing on to moral naturalism.

Herrick's very first story, "An Incurable Disease," limned an egotist of mediocre gifts and secondhand personality who is brought to face his emptiness. With less variation than Herrick perhaps intended, this motif held sway, sometimes verging into stories calling for self-discipline or, in its most positive form, self-realization: the reverential development of one's faculties and genuine talents. But the usual tone was minatory rather than expansive. The earliest story in the Harvard *Monthly*—"Optima and Pessima," printed in May, 1888—warned that "every thought, every sensation" has its "logical predecessor as well as successor," that tiny or seemingly imperceptible actions are laying an unbreakable circuit for the major decisions. This respect for the chain of cause and effect came perhaps from the latest psychology, guided by scientific method rather than by Christian ministers turned academics. More likely, it proved how well Herrick had read the French Naturalists, starting with Balzac. However, it sounded also like George Eliot and, beyond her novels, the Puritan preachers' two-hour demonstration that the smallest sin gives the devil an opening to launch his campaign. In vacillating proportions, Herrick's determinism would always be more moral than social.

Even so, his enthusiasm for the French Naturalists has been underrated. Much as he respected the British and Russian masters of the nineteenth century, his youthful passion locked on the "contemporary French school," which still included the Gustave Flaubert of *Madame Bovary* as well as Émile Zola. As Herrick later stated, he burned to become a "thoroughgoing realist of the modern French type—an American de Maupassant." This testament verged on irony because he had by then concluded that Maupassant "tends to overstress, continually, man's animality" and that, more generally, the Naturalists missed greatness for the same reason. Actually, he had harbored this reservation all along; in the Harvard *Monthly* for June, 1890, his essay on "The Philosophy of a Modern Frenchman" attacked cynical determinism as an approach to human nature. With his stiff-necked ways, the wonder is that he, like Henry James—who got the effect of "a lion in the path"—responded at all to the fleshy, brutal Maupassant.

Only the rare mind has the flexibility to perceive how much hangs on from the god who failed it. Parts of Maupassant's esthetic sank in so deeply that Herrick thought them his own, as worked out in his novels and lecture courses. Furthermore, he would keep giving his French masters credit for turning him against the "sloppily sentimental and romantic" then current (as virtually always) in popular fiction and for emboldening him to "say everything" (in effect, to challenge the most vulnerable taboos). They also taught him the rudiments of objectivity, of the need to suspend his Puritan certitude and merely observe humanity rather than pass judgment. It is hard to see from what other source he could have learned to try, in the aborted novel he wrote after graduating from Harvard in 1890, to make all his characters "dead sure they were individually right." But his full debt can be measured only after going beyond the critical terms of today.

The very term "objective," suggesting for us the author's ability to detach his values from those held by his characters, had for Herrick a more active role, one applied to technique. Roughly synonymous with "dramatic," which is even less understood in this use, it opposed the "analytic," "subjective," or "psychological." It guided the novelists who kept a close rein on preachment, who made action and dialogue carry the theme instead of going minutely into a character's mind and emotions (in pre-Freudian ways). Though not rigidly or unfalteringly, Herrick, as his teaching notes at the University of Chicago in the later 1890's abundantly prove, soon adopted their approach.

Fittingly, these notes are interlarded with citations from "Le Roman," the critical essay Maupassant reprinted as a manifesto for *Pierre et Jean* (1888). From "Le Roman" Herrick took support also for deciding that structure or technique should be unobtrusive, that—more basically—no single method of fiction can claim all the advantages, that the novelist's final goal is to refract the world through his unique temperament, that the most successful Realists are rather "Illusionistes" in imposing their personal vision on their readers, and that the Realist who is truly an artist will achieve not photography but insight. Even in refusing to accept the "slice of life" as a sufficient rationale for fiction, Herrick was agreeing rather than, as some expect, differing with Maupassant.

As a working model, Maupassant's *Bel-Ami* eventually impressed Herrick most of all. Yet his early novels are much closer to the pattern of *Pierre et Jean*, a pattern that once seemed to have the self-evident cogency that he stressed in his teaching. *Pierre et Jean* solidly met the three main desiderata of vivid principals (among them a wife whose younger son was fathered by a lover rather than by her robust but imperceptive husband), a well-defined milieu (of French provincial caution and cunning), and a firm narrative line (in which the other son, stung by a strange legacy to his brother, gouges out the truth).[7] As Herrick would do, to the confusion of those who allow no middle ground between pure terseness and Dickens' elbowing the reader with judgments, Maupassant comments often but holds back at vital points and achieves a progressive revelation. Though Herrick must have winced at the sexual sang-froid, he admired also the absence of sentimentality as the legitimate son is driven into a kind of exile, the strong aura of self-interest cast by everyone, the complexity of motivations, and the refusal to tie up all narrative or plot threads neatly. In "Le Roman" Maupassant argued that endings should leave room for speculation about the remaining years of the characters still alive, an effect Herrick tried hard to achieve in his earlier novels to the sometimes warranted confusion of his public.

V *First Collection of Short Stories*

As yet Herrick had no public, though not for want of trying during the three years he served as an instructor at the Massachusetts Institute of Technology. Frankly, his mind and its concerns deserved no wide hearing before he moved toward profundity by accepting a post at the University of Chicago, where he went in the fall of 1893 to "organize the teaching of rhetoric and composition on the Harvard method." This shift to a cocky, bustling city whose abrasiveness could unsettle the most poised Brahmin was to be attributed to more than thoughtless chance. In another story for the Harvard *Monthly* (of November, 1888), Herrick had noted the economic decline of New England and the "inevitably westward" tide. Besides, the offer from Chicago was professionally attractive as well as flattering. Much later he realized that he had landed at the "only university community in all the world at that time" where his writing career was so fully possible, not only because a then unique quarter system of classwork allowed handier blocks of free months but also because his ambitious president forgave the sins of achievers. As a novelist with faculty tenure, he jumped fifty years ahead of the pattern.

Since the new university was so evidently malleable, with hopes of more millions from John D. Rockefeller before the scaffoldings on the raw

Gothic buildings came down, conflicting advice poured in faster than money. Though given habitually to rocklike stands, Herrick wavered in his attitude to the university between the dignity of a disciple from august Harvard and the pioneer's gusto. In 1895 his view of the university, done for *Scribner's Magazine,* took mostly a very positive note—"Democratic! that is the word we hark back to at every point"—but no students testify to finding him democratic. Many remember an impersonal or haughty lecturer, capable in campus lore of subduing a class impatient to get away to a baseball game with, "Just a moment, if you will be so good; I have a few more pearls to cast." In his weary moods about teaching, Herrick at least avoided pomposity, confessing typically in 1896 to Robert Morss Lovett, who developed at Chicago into a first-rate academic: ". . . the trouble with our work is its arsenical powers on ourselves and its charlatanism toward others." This plaint rose from earned fatigue instead of excuses for loafing at the lectern. No student recorded finding Herrrick lackadaisical or disorganized, especially for his class in advanced composition, which he listed in 1931 as a major interest of his life.

For a while Herrick thought of teaching as his main profession. In solemn essays on questions that faculties still worry with, he mostly defended the quarter system, raised doubts whether freshman writing could be handled best as a separate subject, and deplored emphasis on the "rules" instead of convincing the inarticulate that writing can be "fun." The widely used *Composition and Rhetoric for Schools*—of which he was truly co-author in 1899 for at least the first of its several editions—also stressed the "constructive, stimulative side," valuing effectiveness over empty correctness and appealing to usage over classical authority. Most of his judgments would pass as liberal even on today's campus, and they never toppled into crankiness. His own prose could have profited in several ways from his teachings on rhetoric.

Still, no matter how elevated his esthetic goals might be, he must have thought his writing was going well. Late in 1893 *Scribner's Magazine* accepted two stories, though the *Atlantic Monthly* printed one sooner and thereby appropriately gave another son of Harvard his professional debut. In his high-riding years Herrick sneered often at the author who courts salability, and he did buck many popular ideas many times. But he was excusably eager to start selling in the 1890's. In 1895 he went so far as to try a local-color story, "The Emigration of the Calkins," about a New England family that refuses to leave a township just because the starched folk are so anxious to get rid of it. As his teaching notes reveal, he had no impelling rationale for the short story, despite his reading of Maupassant and occasional gems from Stephen Crane. As a result, editors of the mass-circulation monthlies found his pieces so familiar in essentials that Herrick soon had the backbone of two collections ready to be marketed in the elegantly decorated little volumes that were having their last vogue in the bookstores.

The first, *Literary Love-Letters and Other Stories*, published by Scribner in 1897, was inhabited almost entirely by an upper middle class; most often the setting was a hotel or resort—perhaps because Herrick was traveling enthusiastically on any earnings from his fiction. The stories also made much of romantic love and marriage, though with some unusual touches. As an intertwined theme, they took up artistic temperaments seeking a life style; while uneasy about the esthete, they condemned all signs of the dilettante, for, apparently, only solid achievement excused a taste for the arts. Ironically, Herrick's own art smacked of fin de siècle preciosity despite patches of honest dialogue and motivation.

The title story, cast in talky letters between a cosmopolite worthy of Paul Bourget and a socially ambitious belle whom he finally estranges for their mutual good, reaches a fragile success—almost a walking upon the waters of bathos. The most arresting story—actually, a lyrical dialogue—is the least promising; in "A Prothalamion" the painfully fluent newlyweds, spurning the prospect of nirvana, merely agree that joy would lack dynamic meaning apart from pain and struggle. Herrick's touch in carrying off this flutelike call to strenuosity would soon slip into piercing failures. Likewise, the editors who saw just the right margin of freshness in his patterns soon raised danger signals.

The title of the other volume, *Love's Dilemmas*, published by the new Chicago firm of Stone in 1898, announced a livelier motif for the six stories. Again, the lovers hailed from the middle class or better and were highly articulate—or were exclaimed over for not being so. Yet they gained another degree of vitality over the pairs and triangles of popular fiction as it became apparent that Herrick had no interest in heroines still in their teens emotionally. "A Pension Love Story" ran through a conventional plot—an alert, shrewd bachelor saves an attractive miss from a swindler— only to refuse to ring the wedding bells; it suggested instead that one does not fall in love with a rescuer who all too wisely warns against trouble before it develops.

Sharply unconventional, with burlesque of the standard courtship, "A Temporary Infidelity" had a mannish spinster seduce the affections of an ingénue and then drive away the male suitors. This story went further toward questioning the stereotype of the inviolable maiden than Herrick cared to go again for years. Perhaps he found it, once in print, too much like the worst side of Maupassant, though in the fall of 1897 he asked

Thomas Sergeant Perry, who kept up on continental literature better than any other American, to recommend "any French books, novels or mildly serious," that might help "cultivate" his friends. Perry surely thought that "A Temporary Infidelity" was amply Gallic, especially in its urbanely ironic tone, yet that tone disappeared from Herrick's next work. He must have decided that sophisticated irony could distort his impact almost as sorely as sentimentalism.

VI The Man Who Wins

The decision was sound, for *Love's Dilemmas* could never restore his fame. But *The Man Who Wins* (1897), an unstridently serious novelette published a few months earlier, deserves to be much better known. The first mature upthrust of his Realism, it achieves a starkly simple, hard-hitting effect through Jarvis Thornton, a young physician fascinated by research and, incidentally, a very early example of the Martin Arrowsmith syndrome. Thorton, attracted partly by a physical undertow to a daughter of a decadent family, is inexorably forced into moneymaking to satisfy her obligations and habits. When his own daughter grows up, Thornton, with objectivity rather than self-pity, dissuades a talented artist from drifting toward a similar mismatch. Quietly expounding the difference between "succeed" and "win," between making good in the world's practical eye and devotion to one's highest values, the father—too easily—talks the painter into accepting his subsidy for study in Paris; presumably, the daughter will turn to somebody else with no sharp pain. Readers who expected a consoling denouement, if only immortal fame for the artist, were left waiting.

Besides defying the addiction for domestic pathos, *The Man Who Wins* looked with American tenacity at what constitutes success—a question answered more soothingly by Howells' bluff Silas Lapham just as Herrick was getting ready for Harvard. In Herrick's novel, the businessman has shrunk to John Ellwell and his son, plungers in the market who were tipsily completing the cycle from "Shirtsleeves to Shirtsleeves," the title of one of Herrick's undergraduate manuscripts, according to Lovett. *The Man Who Wins*—though dedicated to his wife with whom he virtually eloped in 1894, despite sound reasons to love elsewhere—also confirmed Herrick's enlistment in the war between the sexes, one not yet so widely noted as to have earned that name. Thornton warns his daughter's admirer: ". . . if she were normal or dull, not an exacting young American, yet she would be a woman. And as such her interest must be opposed to yours forever" (120–21). This warning later expanded into the impassioned theme of *The*

Healer (1911); at present, Herrick diluted it with still other themes, such as the fate of the New England tradition. Thornton's olympian father, indirectly blessing Herrick's move to Chicago, discourses on "degenerate" Puritan families whose "stock was too fine bred in and in" and whose wisest scions "scattered themselves forty years ago into new lands."

But the best case for *The Man Who Wins* rests on the tautly complex personalities. The physician's relations with his daughter stand comparison with the roughly similar set in *Washington Square*, in which Henry James's subtlety is blurred by surface comedy and condescension. Herrick, trusting in a quietly polished style, rewrote more carefully than he would usually do again, suppressing not only the comic but the genteel pose. One reviewer praised the "effort to avoid pedantry,"[8] for this spareness of style was joined with honesty of detail; and its effect on both the diction and the content of the dialogue is best illustrated during a dinner party at the Ellwell home. Increasingly sordid facts, unadorned by righteous scolding, made the decline of the Ellwells graphic and credible.

This novelette proved to be Herrick's most objective piece of fiction; besides avoiding intrusions, his impersonal narrator kept out of the actors' minds as much as he could while still getting the plot told. Objectivity took over the main effect from the Naturalistic touches of determinism or man's animality, even if they showed the power of environment and heredity so well that it overshadowed the area Herrick left for free will.[9] *The Man Who Wins* reached close to fitting Herrick's dream of becoming an American Maupassant, though for that the ending needed a deeper shade of gloom. Still, the family in Boxford on whom the Ellwells were reputedly patterned had full cause for their dudgeon.

VII *Maturity as a Novelist*

All of his career Herrick leaned too much on real-life models, with the curious yet common result that his characters too often seem smaller than humanity. Somewhat boorishly, his first full-fledged novel, *The Gospel of Freedom* (1898), based a leading figure on his college friend and recent host in Italy, Bernard Berenson, who had already begun his climb to eminence as an art critic-historian. But nobody has found a transparent source for the roundly imagined heroine, Adela Anthon, who is far different from any other woman in Herrick's short stories. Though also of the upper middle class with her inheritance of eighteen thousand dollars a year and greater expectations, she is a New Woman, a role that dwarfs her similarities to James's Isabel Archer, whose name she echoes.

Adela thinks hard and often about the female's place in the power structure and about her relations with its captains; she proves that her creator had continued to profit from the growing influence of Ibsen, which accelerated in the late 1880's with English translations, from reputable publishers, of such controversial plays as *A Doll's House* and *An Enemy of the People*. Adela, first attracted to a rising financier because he had accepted her as a business "partner," rebels at being forced into ornamental superficiality by the routine expected of a Chicago lake-shore matron. Breaking with her baffled husband, she seeks fulfillment in the ateliers and galleries of Europe; not in flight from sex, she still hopes vaguely to make a true Ibsenish marriage in which she will function as an equal. Herrick managed her search for compatability with such dignity that he was able to get by without further pretence at plot or subplot and even without the coincidences or loud crises of popular fiction.

In grappling with the New Woman suddenly freed from the "gospel of work," Herrick looked deeper than either of the popular approaches—idealization and paternalism. Dedicating her, as a swarm of ephemeral writers were doing, to the guardianship of spiritual values, could not satisfy him, possibly because of his mother's baneful greeds; he never belittles Adela for wanting to take a practical hand in business; and her foil, Molly Parker, shares her fiancé's reformist crusades. Nor could Herrick follow the approach of condescension; he lets Adela gain insight without leaning on male advice or being bailed out of her divorce by a sedate remarriage. At the end of the novel, she rejects the expatriate circles of Europe not from maidenly disdain but from the elemental discovery that the Americans she left behind "have my blood, the self-same inheritance with me. In them and with them must I make my life, if it is to be anything." For the immediate present, she goes home to look after her narrow, prattling mother; but she is accepting her obligations rather than expiating her willful mistakes. Having renounced the dream of far-flung independence only to declare bravely at the close, "I must learn to live," she ends with enhanced dignity even if she is merely starting all over. In a favorable review, Howells could not resist citing the quip that "when an American woman loses her innocence she goes and gets some more," skeptically adding that "in some such way" Adela "saves herself."[10] Just how she is to live more wisely is indeed left open, more from Herrick's lack of a solution than from his dislike of rounding off his story too neatly.

Still, strenuously distinct from the dourness of a Maupassant, Ibsen had lately announced in a fresh battery of plays that living is an endless struggle in which even the wisest decisions bring fresh difficulties. His influence burned much deeper than is today generally understood, when many voices are questioning the dream of stasis. Furthermore, in Herrick's *The Gospel of Freedom*, Ibsenism goes beyond Adela's rejection of an ornamental role and her discovery of sobering human duty. Through her husband's lake-shore clique, she discovers that the "pillars of society" are often corrupt, that its leaders may cynically exploit their power. Soon Herrick also echoed Ibsen in showing how their power can undermine artistic and professional integrity or how the overlords of respectability can ostracize the idealist who challenges their mores by deed or by speaking the disruptive truth.

Young Herrick had already become his own master, nevertheless, in transmuting Ibsen through distinctively American patterns. Like Henry James, Herrick used wealthy heroines because their margin of disposable freedom allowed a sharper look at the choices raised by an affluent economy. Fifteen years later, in his first attempt at autobiography, he decided that the largest issue in *The Gospel of Freedom* had been the "struggle between the individual's desire for personal liberty and the conditions of life." Occasionally, Adela simplified this desire into a hunger for "experience" over a wider spectrum than that sanctioned by her genteel status as the beneficiary of her father's gospel of work. Yet she was essentially driven by the broader, spreading hunger incited by the mounting profits in the New World; escape from the grind of making ends meet opened up the liberty of pursuing happiness full-time and the hope of capturing it totally.

Unhobbled by the religious heritage, however undoctrinal, of an Isabel Archer, Adela—who squelches her "sallow-faced . . . awkward" pastor—is one of the first adults in American fiction who expect, even demand, to be vigorously happy in the urban garden of plenty. Of course, any reader who knows Herrick's Puritan heritage knows what it will decide: we cannot escape sacrifice or our responsibility to "accept the world as it comes to our hands, to shape it painfully without regard for self,—that brings the soul to peace" (267). No other way can quiet the soul, not even the increasingly esteemed pursuit of culture or—as Herrick sneered—of the "dainties" of European art and tradition.

Unexpectedly cool toward intellect, whether devoted to business or art criticism, the novel scrutinized the soundness of esthetic hedonism. Herrick particularly meant to attack "ultra estheticism," which struck him as a debased and attenuated Puritanism in which spirituality thinned into preciousness. Likewise, he was debating the value of creation against subtilized appreciation; perhaps he was troubled by his pull between writing and teaching and, less personally, by whether gusto or meticulous analysis served his classes in literature better. Simeon Erard, painter and essayist on old masterpieces in the novel, raises the issue compellingly even while again and again proving his keen, informed competence.

In one of the common ironies befalling novelists, Herrick outdid himself with Erard; and his character intrigued readers who had never heard of Berenson. The reader is, therefore, more reluctant than Herrick to turn away from Erard's expertise and agree with the summary judgment: "Life is not fulfilled, we are not quieted, in that way" (267). This rejection would at least have greater force if the novel convincingly acted out its aversion for the lesser devotees of appreciation, the "dilettantes . . . little artists, lazy scholars." Herrick was in fact exorcising his lifelong fear, like Nathaniel Hawthorne's, of becoming a cold, sterile intellectual. While not basically moving away from esthetic values, he must have been telling himself to live more fully and less cerebrally. Molly Parker, Adela's satellite but emotional superior, is a noble savage in bombazine; warm, spontaneous, and happy, she has no worries about being otherwise.

The lesson lived by nonverbal Molly is stated by her fiancé, who counsels Adela that freedom, a "feeling you cannot command," "takes us unawares when we have given up the search." Without going so far as the bridegroom in "A Prothalamion," who finds the "same gift of life" as much in a "railroad carried through" as in a great painting, he also states the wisdom of cleaving to the realm of flesh and blood; he insists at the end of the story that if "I were merely going to rot, I should rather rot with the Philistines and be a good human animal" and that Erard's clique was "nearer dead" than the bruising financiers of Chicago (264). This pronouncement is apparently the last word, though Adela had found that the ways of turning a fat profit got less palatable the more she saw them from the inside and though Herrick had intruded to condemn Chicago as a makeshift and ugly shell for materialistic goals. In the last analysis, Herrick had just begun to make up his mind about that city and, more largely, was still wrestling as hard as Adela with how to live. The philistines were soon to rage against what he thought he had learned.

But mature novels deal less in answers than in basic questions of conduct as they are refracted through individuals who face them painfully and seldom with unflawed glory. *The Gospel of Freedom* comes close to maturity beneath its unpretentious tone and firmly objective method. Those who measure by the bleakest standard of objectivity may fail to see how well Herrick reins in the obtrusive author. This especially applies to Erard, whose mind is never entered very far; but, too accomplished for us to dismiss him as a poseur, he emerges as a unique personage, a gritty paradox whose satanic cunning interweaves with his devotion to the arts, whose self-respect easily sheds the climactic rebuff from Adela. Most of the other characters are likewise rendered as honestly as Emma Bovary's neighbors—Adela's vapid mother, the harmlessly disagreeable and snobbish brother, Adela herself. If details waver, Adela's portrait nevertheless has balance; and it ranges to include an irrational streak she cannot tame and a conscious trick of acting haughty when ill at ease. No character, as Herrick should have noted for his future guidance as an artist, undergoes sudden conversion, no crisis seems forced, no neat verdict falls on every head.

Barely thirty, Herrick had progressed rapidly as a writer. In 1935, Joseph Wood Krutch still remembered the "absolute greatness" that he "seemed as a young man to promise"; but Krutch probably had in mind the next novel or two after *The Gospel of Freedom*. But, as late as 1909, Howells thought it his "greatest book." Appearing at a time when, Howells felt, the soft romancers were regaining prestige, Herrick's novel led Realism toward harsher heights. We would be narrowly truthful but also evasive in considering it a transitional work; for, in a slightly different sense, so are most great novels. If Herrick has intrinsic worth, *The Gospel of Freedom* must stand as the earliest proof of it. Yet a crucial omen lurked in a minor detail: he failed to reach emotional intimacy or even a first-name basis with his heroine. Herrick never reached uninhibited rapport with his later characters, including those heroes modeled after himself. Though his first novel gave grounds for hope, the human warmth of the most compelling fiction would always elude him.

CHAPTER 2

The Full Range

I *Feelings toward the Chicago School*

Herrick's habit of addressing his heroines formally lasted through several more novels, but the reserve that made him outdo even the punctilious Henry James on this score lasted much longer. In 1920, when we were on the brink of an era of mass cordiality, he exclaimed: "How I dislike our modern habit of intimate address! "[1] Going beyond his desire to oppose Rotarian excess, his reserve often assumed the manners of a snob. His old and loyal crony Lovett has confirmed the many anecdotes to that effect, conceding that he was "extremely fastidious" and that "etiquette meant much to him." If this side of Herrick showed at its worst in the year or two after he had arrived to uplift the new University of Chicago toward a Harvard tone, success as a writer did little to erode it; but, nonetheless, he always managed to hold friends of genuine depth and warmth.

Herrick's aloofness went so far as to keep him out of the last cycle of the "clubs" for gentlemen, which Chicago tried to copy from London by way of the Eastern cities. As a bachelor, he had enough pent-up chatter to help start the "windbag," a circle of fellow teachers who for a while clamored at a beer garden near the campus. But he shunned the array of downtown groups, formal to informal, that had sprung up in the name of the arts. Above all, he ambitiously scorned being part of any Chicago "school," and he invariably foiled Hamlin Garland's attempts to recruit him for the campaign to seize the leadership of culture for the Midwest. Although Herrick sometimes read the local novelists, he gave them no worthwhile support; and he lacked any appreciation for strolling reporters like George Ade or newspaper satirists like Finley Peter Dunne, who were savoring the clatter of the streets and the plebeian color that were missing in Herrick's fiction. As for the Bohemia of the marginal man, his fastidiousness raised an impermeable curtain. At the other pole, incidentally, his ambitious wife failed to involve him with high society, though she unwittingly passed on some clues about its brash mores.

At the heart of his literary seclusiveness lay two attitudes, once stated most clearly years later in a letter to Malcolm Cowley: "I avoided instinctively the patter and chatter about letters and art, the literary 'schools' already forming in the Nineties. I avoided as a rule contacts with men of my two professions, teaching and writing, preferring the talk of a drummer in a Pullman or a sailor on a boat to the conversations about Art and Life."[2]

As The *Gospel of Freedom* proved, he stayed cool from the start to the current form of "art for art's sake," later insisting that it belonged to the "individualistic debauch" that culminated in the crash of 1929; he was downright grim over the lurid fallout from Oscar Wilde's American tour in 1882, which included a melee at Harvard, and the sensational trial in 1893. Also, as his first novel indicated, he mistrusted the archpriests of high culture as sterile (Erard has little sexuality) and narcissistic; on a more mundane level, he felt, all too rightly, a need for richer contact with the daily parade than they gave.

However, his claim of literary isolation missed the truth in several ways. His years in the coterie around the Harvard *Monthly* had been invaluable; similarly, he was getting more light and heat from his colleagues at the new university than he realized, with vicarious dabbling in broader streams added through Lovett. He escaped the typical agony of the young American writer of his time—marooned in a small town, condescendingly suspect by the philistines, ripe for some eccentric revelation. Finally, he did belong to the Chicago school in some ways—as an extension student if nothing else.

Chicago was, far more than any other place, his home during thirty years of writing in which, too slavishly for the liking of both friends and enemies, he drew on his current experiences. Just as inescapably, Chicago was the big city he knew best, indeed knew first, since his Cambridge then seemed farther from Boston than the actual miles. The urban problem could not have loomed so large or actively disturbing in his structure of values if Chicago had not battered his ears and eyes. Its assaults gained intensity from the fact that it was Midwestern, alien to a Yankee and unruled by the codifications bred into him. In turn, it had as yet no hardened image for its natives. Herrick not only could do his own generalizing but was forced to, with a sense of groping for patterns and with an anxiety that, as Floyd Dell liked to repeat, "Chicago is not a place where stories happen." Not the stories of hackneyed romance anyway, for Herrick eventually perceived that the city had pressed upon him the "world of fact" and, in particular, the roar of the competitive scramble breaking through the moral clichés.

His reactions toward Chicago grew as complex and tortured as the world of fact itself. The simplest pattern of reaction was cyclical. Usually he disliked Chicago when in residence there, tied to his teaching schedule and the distractions of interoffice memos. Yet, soon after he escaped, he started yearning to go back and pick up a solid routine, to trade the rootlessness of travel for duties in the workaday world. In spite of opportunities to settle elsewhere, he regularly came home to Chicago, more pleased than he admitted with its clamor and its ambitious schemes. Having freely elected to move to the West, he sent many of his characters on the same road, not to evade problems but to find a broader, lustier scope. After the first few years, he never bemoaned his exile from Cambridge and never threatened to join an expatriate colony, either urban or primitive. During the years he was willing to live in a city, he decided it might as well be Chicago.

Cutting across the cycle of escape and return, his more reflective attitudes evolved along with inner and outer events. Because the Midway of the great fair of 1893 was still blaring on his arrival, he tended to overreact against local gloating and to find the Midwest as crude as he had feared. Almost perversely, when its euphoria dimmed into such troubles as the Pullman strike, he found heart for a kinder tone; and, in his sketch of the new university for *Scribner's Magazine*, he declared: "The people of Chicago are eager, in a sense that is true nowhere else in our country, for art, literature, education, the accompaniments of a complex civilization." Then he settled down to a tense ambivalence, jarred by Chicago's lusty "commercialism" but quickened by its bluff vitality. The protagonists in four of his first five novels end there after fleeing to try for solutions elsewhere. In 1905 he clipped from the local *Evening Post* a feature article, by an old Harvard friend, which asserted that Herrick had got over his determination to "civilize" Chicago and now admired it as a "real thing, a more vigorous entity than any of our eastern cities." However, if not overstated, this acceptance was the high-water mark; for beginning with *Together* in 1908, his heroes, who earlier turned to nature only for guidance in a crisis, increasingly rejected the modern city, no matter which one.

II *A Height of Realism*

Before entering that stage, his novels showed Chicago in many poses, especially in *The Web of Life* (1900). Not much of the portrait there was favorable, though it demanded respect for Colonel Hitchcock, presented as typical of the generation of merchants who had built Chicago into a center of trade. The first notes for the novel called for also including a "tranquil, high-minded capitalist, who has inherited large wealth, who spends it beautifying his city, enriching it, who loves to give, who is probity and honor and sagacity." These last three virtues were transferred to Colonel Hitchcock, but he was too secondary to keep local newspapers from belaboring *The Web of Life* for raking deep into sore spots such as the public-school system. The president of the board of education hastily issued a rejoinder; several anonymous voices chimed in with personal attacks on Herrick. His wife, an ally of the country-club and charity-ball set which also took offence, felt obliged to insist publicly that her husband was "friendly" toward Chicago. The chesty metropolis on the lake had proved just as touchy as Gopher Prairie was to be.

Much more perceptively, a critic for the London *Spectator* remarked that Herrick had written as if "there were no other place than Chicago in the world." Though Herrick was too cosmopolitan in his aims to treasure this astute judgment, he had made Chicago oppressively concrete, both as a historical backdrop and as a physical setting. The action of *The Web of Life* interweaves with public events, picking up force along with the Pullman strike and closing soon after the end of the Spanish-American War. The first personal crisis of its hero, the physician Howard Sommers, coincides with the strike; too ironically, his worst struggles come in an abandoned "temple" that was once a booth at the gleaming fair; after an exile in New York City, he returns to Chicago with some of its bedraggled crusaders against Spain. History aside, the setting is very much localized with the lake-shore mansions, the climbing skyline, the jerrybuilt boarding houses, and the ragged prairie at the end of the streetcar lines as well as, more casually, the stockyards, railroad web, and the Midway. In its raw grandeur and grime, this Chicago is usually closer to the average truth than the exciting mecca of Theodore Dreiser's *Sister Carrie*.

Herrick's novel also has a firmer cross-section of classes and cliques, though the plot marches onward as simply as Dreiser's. Sommers, too sincere to accept the smug clichés of the wealthy or their largesse, turns away from the society girl he is tacitly courting in the early chapters; he also rejects with gusto the foothold that her family has arranged in a fashionable clinic. In due time and with slow molding by events, his rebellion carries him into living with Alves Preston, the widow of an alcoholic whose life he had prolonged with his medical talent. After additional events create a series of defeats, Alves—whom Herrick does call by her first name, unlike her high-placed rival, Louise Hitchcock—commits suicide because the grind for their subsistence is wasting Sommers' gifts. After a decent amount of added trials, he proposes at last to his first love but stipulates that he will accept little of her father's money and will earn a modest income as an "old-fashioned" physician. In summary, this plot sounds more sentimental than Herrick allows it to become in tone. *The Web of Life* challenges many stereotypes and asks more questions than he could answer. Retrospectively, he conceded that his hero attains only a "rather lame sort of reconciliation with life."

Most prominent among the unanswered questions in *The Web of Life* was one already left dangling by *The Gospel of Freedom*, one most acute in a rich, open society: to what extent can men be vibrantly happy and untrammeled? With an Ibsenish undertone, Alves, like Molly Parker in the preceding novel, lives by a high-minded yet gently primitive code of "joy." But she is borne down by innocence, chance, and the group's mores, leaving Sommers as the fullest case for judgment. He begins by sanguinely rejecting the help of the well-placed as constrictive and as unfair to his competitors. However, he finds that he cannot get far single-handed, that following his professional ideals brings little praise and less income, that "self-made men are generally lucky men, who have had the right friends," that it is wrong to try to avoid entangling responsibilities or to set himself apart from the "multitude." For the moment, Herrick finally relents; he lets his hero find a muted freedom and contentment but the duty of sharing the common lot would soon trouble Herrick more tenaciously.

The fiercest light of *The Web of Life* trained on the related question of success. Its modern price, Herrick both suggested and preached, added up to the loss of principle through crawling for the favors of the powerful and trampling down the weak or finicky—a "brutal" creed (201–2). Once bought, success entailed additional corruption not only for its heirs, like Louise Hitchcock's brother who perhaps will more suavely go the way of Alves's husband, but also for its captains. With hardening arrogance they gather into an elite who stifle individuality, exploit the young who are anxious to join them, and crush their enemies through the police and the courts.

The Web of Life struck at the rich, especially the banker and big operator in stocks, more tellingly than any American novel had done before. It just about as harshly attacked the labor unions, whose leaders sell out when the price gets right. Nevertheless, along with this decrying of a cash standard, Herrick seemed to be calling for nothing more radical than a completely open race, as when Sommers, denying that he favors "fine theories about social service and all that settlement stuff," demands only a "man's right to start with the crowd at the scratch" (196). Going back to the starting blocks, then, in a pure laissez-faire spirit was the most specific remedy Herrick had found so far for the turmoil of success and the war between the classes, which *The Web of Life* saw as under way. At least the recourse to a fresh start, to beginning all over again, proved him much more American than his local enemies were calm enough to perceive.

Never sure about his scale of what a novel may encompass, Herrick had tried more in this novel than he was capable of managing. Also, his desire to lay open all evasions gives *The Web of Life* a querulous effect, an air of picking flaws everywhere. Because he was in part decisively uncommitted,

Herrick meant rather, like Eugene O'Neill, to suggest a tortured groping; he had Sommers sigh with earned humility toward the end, "No man knows what he is doing—to any great extent" (328). The last chapter, likewise, deftly suggests that the struggle for insight and equilibrium will snare each new generation in a web of hungers, ideals, and frustrations. Before a man gets far toward understanding himself and his world, he has reached the grave while humanity is ceaselessly spawning more strugglers. This somber affirmation of an inscrutable vitality agreed surprisingly well with Dreiser's *Sister Carrie*, which was published in the same year.

Besides this chord—and the Chicago setting—the two novels had many other points of similarity. Like Carrie Meeber, Alves is a Wisconsin farm girl who is soon taken in by a "city slicker" whom she outgrows. Just as patently as Carrie, she violates the sexual code; in his notes Herrick debated having her and Sommers "live together before the husband's death," but he decided to wait until the night after the funeral; then they set up housekeeping without any legal rites. A scene in which Alves, "thoughtfully" eyeing her body, "unbuttoned and unlaced" down to the "nakedness and simplicity of life" and then asked Sommers, "Do you like me? " goes further than the "decolleté" one reviewer deplored and is franker than any episode allowed Carrie. To be sure, Alves did not enjoy the continuing good fortune that enraged Carrie's censors. Still, Herrick refused to appease morality in other closing touches: neither Sommers nor Dresser, the labor leader who sold out, nor Parker Hitchcock, an elegant loafer, is punished according to devout standards. Furthermore, Herrick at this stage had probed more keenly than Dreiser into the heart of the power structure.

This comparison does not lead to the conclusion that Herrick had written a greater novel than *Sister Carrie*; it serves mainly to suggest that 1900 was a vintage year for American fiction, one honored also by Robert Grant's *Unleavened Bread*, which as austerely refused to curry moral favor while dissecting a society matron and a time-serving politician. However, Herrick's very ambition to write fiction worthy of joining the masterpieces he praised in his university classes kept him from matching Dreiser's ruggedly plain, low-keyed handling of scene and motive. Herrick had early grown eager, Lovett recalls, to get "passion" into his pages. Unable to anticipate William Faulkner's techniques for emotional resonance, he blurred his starkly conceived characters with bombast and melodramatic lapses. Though a chain of chance meetings tends to make his Chicago seem no bigger than the Palmer House lobby, the fault ran deeper than an onsetting weakness for coincidence. Sound in intention, he often made Sommers act convincingly as an idealist who can nonetheless be tough, as when he bullies Mrs. Ducharme—a brilliant vignette of fecklessness and animality—into leaving Chicago forever. But too often Sommers deafens the mind as he declaims in eloquent, excited, yet heavily abstract rhetoric.

Although worse prose lay ahead as in the painful climax in *A Life for a Life*, any sensitive reader of today writhes under a cadenza by the reputedly inarticulate Alves:

"You can hear it in the night air," she murmured; "the joy that comes rising up from the earth, the joy of living. Ah! that is why we are made—to have happiness and joy, to rejoice the heart of God, to make God live, for *He* must be happiness itself; and when we are happy and feel joy in living, He must grow stronger. And when we are weak and bitter, when the world haunts us . . . when men strike and starve, and others are hard and grasping—then He must shrink and grow small and suffer. There *is* happiness," she ended, breathing her belief as a prayer into the solitude and night. (164)

Still numbed by a tradition of inflated dialogue, Herrick lacked Dreiser's sense of how few and simple are the phrases some people use, no matter what the occasion. Likewise, he became too verbose about the silent rapport that Alves and Sommers achieve far too soon. Eventually, he learned that understatement best served his principle that the objective method is the "more scientific, the more artistic perhaps." But *The Web of Life* strained to communicate point and passion, with most harm to the effect Sommers makes. At least, this verbosity usually stayed out of the private musings of the other characters, thereby keeping Louise Hitchcock intriguingly taciturn.

Herrick's dialogue also fell into an inconsistency that had long marred British and American fiction. While his well-bred heroes orate, the plebeians often sound idiomatic. Thus, Mrs. Ducharme mumbles convincingly about her troubles with witch doctors; unlike Alves, her husband rings true as he whines, "I need a little whiskey to keep me going. Tell her, won't you? —to let me have a little drink. My regular allowance was a pint a day, and I haven't had a drop for four weeks." It must have been such passages that reviewers had in mind when they noted that the "shadow" of Henry James did not "appear at all" in *The Web of Life*, or that Flaubert's did. Though Herrick, in looking back, labeled much of his early work as "drab realism," he probably hoped this novel rather challenged comparison with Émile Zola.

III *A Height of Idealism*

Dissatisfied with *The Web of Life*, as well as its reception, though not ashamed of either, he reverted in *The Real World* (1901) to the handier scale of his first novel, which had more of the workmanlike directness of Howells than the intricacies of James. Unfortunately, *The Real World* was stodgier in some ways than the evolving practices of the now elderly Howells, to whom Herrick gave surprisingly little notice in his classes. Again the heroine remained "Miss Mather" until her wedding day, though a less patrician lady became "Elsie" to the omniscient narrator. The idiomatic touch in the dialogue still wavered, with slang still exiled almost entirely to the plebeians. At least the narrative style made a distinct improvement through its steady pace and calmer tone; on this count, one heavily scored against him in the years ahead, Herrick could presently savor praise for a "distinctly virile straightforwardness" that never verged on "fustian."[3]

But the over-all structure of *The Real World* was routinely wooden. For no compelling reason it starts at the middle of Jack Pemberton's boyhood, moves him through adolescence with too little élan, promotes him to earned success in the city, has him abandon his law practice as stifling, and closes by sending him—wed finally to the rich girl he had admired since his days in ragged knickers—to help direct risky but constructive dealings in the West. Despite Maupassant's advice not to strain at tying up the loose ends, virtually nobody drops out of sight, and Jack sooner or later gets even with anybody who ever looked down on him.

This vengefulness was apparently irresistible because Jack's career drew on Herrick's youth—it opens with the most dolorous episode of his own boyhood, details the jangling insecurity in his household, and transmutes only somewhat more loosely Herrick's experiences as Jack moves into work at a summer hotel where the patrons keep him aware of his inferiority even as one of them, Elsie Mason, encourages him to aim for Harvard. Similarly, the Harvard episodes, as Jack slowly acquires self-confidence and a profession, retrace Herrick's inner growth or else borrow from that of the revered Philip Abbot, after whom he named his first son. Though Jack is a budding lawyer rather than an artist, Herrick was anticipating the revival of the *Bildungsroman*. Without the extremes of terror and nostalgia in James Joyce or in Sherwood Anderson, he conveyed the same bittersweet aura of longing and ambition. And less consciously than Thomas Wolfe's *Look Homeward, Angel*, but as doggedly, Herrick worked off many old resentments.

The name that Herrick first preferred for his *Bildungsroman* was *Jock O' Dreams*. Impatient because the uneasy reviews of his first two novels had missed his basic points, he wanted to make them plainer now. The epigraph for *The Web of Life* had called man both angel and demon; this tension between higher and lower nature ran more clearly and prominently through *The Real World*. On Herrick's conscious level, the longings of youth were only a pivot for this tension, which he treated not within the rising sympathy for the myth of innocence and initiation but within the brief vogue of attempting to fuse Realism with the moral strenuosity still potent in most quarters. Frank Norris, whose career ended prematurely in 1902, tried the same path, one which even guided Dreiser's *Sister Carrie* into passages preaching the hope of eventual spirituality.

The idealistic side of *The Real World* is so evident that it would be easy to overlook the counterweights. But "drab realism," as Herrick ambivalently labeled it, dominates characters like a sickly waitress at the Maine resort or a threadbare student of the Classics. Others, especially the mistress of Jack's brother or her friend Liddy, break the limits of Howellsian truth-telling; the Chicago *Tribune* reviewer, disposed to be hostile because of *The Web of Life*, calculated that "out of the nine women who figure in the book five were unchaste." Liddy maneuvers to get Jack up to her bedroom soon after they meet, and Elsie Mason confesses prophetically, "I feel hard as nails some days. I feel I could do anything to get what I wanted." Along with further sexual notes, the employees at the hotel hold a picnic enlivened with beer while Elsie's summering circle has a champagne party with at least one drunk draped on the floor. The most sustained stretch of Realism involves a bruising campaign by ruthless speculators with no mercy for weakness, but they are tamer than Dreiser's survival-of-the-fittest financiers in his Cowperwood novels yet to be written.

Intrepidly, the action of the novel aimed to generate equal force for a realm shining above the mundane. According to Lovett, a "vein of mysticism" ran to the vital center of Herrick, who once acclaimed *The Real World* as his favorite. Besides trying to make higher nature triumph convincingly, it all too explicitly insists on the gulf between the physical and the spiritual, often with images of a light-dark or mist-sunshine polarity and with plays on the meaning of "real" assumed by those dumb to the emotion and value beyond the "indifferent shades of mere appearance" (16, 27, 86, 169, 187, 326). Yet, though the intangible sphere is vastly superior, and much less in correspondence with brute reality than Emerson had hoped, Herrick was not rejecting the gross world. Instead, he was warning, if without recourse to even the attenuated religious sanctions of the Victorians, that men's finest qualities depend on their piercing through the tyranny of the senses in order to steer by nobly chosen concepts. What his metaphysics lacked in system, he compensated for in emphasis.

As is usual, idealism for Herrick entailed ethical standards—which were somewhat more precise. Loyal to his provenance, he made his spokesman a New Englander who learns at Harvard that "to live finely was the best thing in life, better than honor and fame and success" (142–43). If readers of Herrick's first novels had understood at all, they were expecting in this novel the capping lesson that the main instrument for living finely is the will. It sustains Jack Pemberton through a ladder of ordeals and it waxes stronger with each experience and rarifies its touch. It proves fatally weak in Jack's long-suffering father and self-indulgent brother, who helps to teach us that the "will, rightly organized and directed, is the means by which we attain the knowledge of reality. Misdirected and enfeebled, it is also the means whereby we sink deeper into illusion."[4] The early twentieth century brought much lay preaching about the will as a manipulating and even cognitive tool—just before the full impact of Freud put idealists on the defensive. While Herrick had as yet little chance to read Nietzsche, he inevitably heard about Theodore Roosevelt's glorification of personal force. Still, as his next novel, *The Common Lot*, showed best, he was also too swayed by the claims of our shared nature to make Jack a superman except, some cynics might say, in self-denial.

Whatever the spreading rumors of Herrick's philandering, he believed that self-denial must rigorously channel the will. In *The Real World* its enemy is physical appetite more than convention or inertia. Perhaps in self-reproach, sex emerges as the main lure away from finely oriented action. Passion hurried Jack's father into a stultifying marriage; after spurning two lesser Circes, even Jack is sorely tempted by Elsie Mason, who had given moral support while he was working his way through Harvard and then was climbing as an attorney in New York City. Touched by Jack's years of quiet devotion and bored with her marriage for money, Elsie decides to seduce him with tantalizingly staged overtures. But Jack tears away from pulsating Elsie, who incidentally belies a reviewer's complaint that characters in *The Real World* have "very little temperament." As his lust is controlled, he discovers that he has gained full mastery of his will, rising forever above those who "with each pang of the striving nerves . . . lost the power to possess." He at once discovers also—in the words of Herrick's working notes—that "passion restrained goes to make great power." This computing of virtue, which Freudians might assess in dismaying ways, sounded more like Tennyson's Galahad than a successful lawyer.

When Jack had achieved mastery of the appetites, he had to be depicted as practicing it. Herrick's Realistic side demanded this exercise but at the same time made it hard to do; as a result, the ending chapters are unconvincing. In them Herrick opted for program over credibility; he swaps Jack's legal career for a plunge into business deals which—the working notes mused—"will take him out of dreams into a very real world, will allay the feeling of unreality." But, exploiting the classic evasion for American writers, Herrick sent Jack out to the plains and spared him the impossible ordeal of coercing monopolistic trusts and the stock market to obey the spirit. On a last island of frontier, he delays confrontation with the J. P. Morgans by helping to whip a needed railroad into order.

Herrick was unjust to *The Real World* in closing it so stodgily. In spite of Jack's heroics, it sometimes attained effective comedy. At its best, it quietly set down the ironies of fumbling judgment, such as the faith that a bedraggled mistress has in Jack's spineless brother; it also had flashes of gentle satire, such as her taste for crème de menthe or at most a "nice tintsy, wintsy cocktail." As his short stories promised and future novels proved, Herrick could develop serious ideas with a light touch. The opening scene of his next book, the novelette *Their Child* (1903), made apt use of drawing-room badinage and a "large, very blonde, very well preserved" sophisticate "known by her intimates as the 'Magnificent Wreck.' " Yet his intentions were still too feverish to tolerate humor for long.

If we remember Herrick's early vow to avoid courting public taste, to have an audience on his "own terms or none at all," it is hard to see why Herrick bothered to write *Their Child*. Heavily sentimental after the first scene, it centers on a five-year-old boy, handsome of course, who has inherited a homicidal mania through his father; after threatening to destroy the parents' rapport, this problem draws them closer together than before. Perhaps the plot held private relief for Herrick; his marriage had been floundering for several years; furthermore, his first child proved mentally and physically defective, leaving Herrick guilty about having married his first cousin. This charitable reading does not explain why the editors for Macmillan, which published virtually all of his books between 1898 and 1914, accepted *Their Child*. If they did so merely to keep him from defecting, the many favorable reviews were clearer reward than publishers usually get for such sacrifices.

One reviewer cast light on both the genesis and reception of *Their Child* by noting that "atavism" or "heredity" was a fad; for the rest of his life Herrick would fret about eugenics and, occasionally, "race suicide." In this same vein, another critic discovered that Herrick was "evidently a student" of Ibsen, particularly of his *Ghosts*—then a notorious "problem play" about an inherited neural disease. Less shrewdly, another found the novelette a "tablet of compressed Zolaism," thinking perhaps of the dinner party in *Their Child* at which the distraught father gets drunk on champagne, roars out a stag-party song, and lurches away for lustier fun without his wife. Nearest to the mark for us was the critic who detected the influence of Maupassant, probably because of the subplot in *Their Child* in which a former suitor of the wife rushes to exploit the temporary rift. Echoing one last time the idol of his apprenticeship, Herrick conducted this nasty byplay with taut economy and understatement; but the main influence behind it came from a genteel public avid for heartrending dilemmas of family life.

IV *A Middle Ground*

Healthier sides of current taste responded warmly to Herrick's next novel, *The Common Lot* (1904), which was attractive enough to the publisher to be serialized in the *Atlantic Monthly*. A pivotal segment of the middle class was finally discerning flaws in the workings of laissez-faire economics, such as its failure to spread wealth as broadly as it had promised. Against the grain of his Puritan individualism, Herrick had started to face that failure. Simeon Erard's father suffered on a back street of Jersey City; *The Web of Life* noticed the gaunt or threadbare more often; and many farmers of Maine and Iowa in *The Real World* needed better food and clothes. In the new novel, Sayre Coburn, a physician researching in his grimy quarters, refuses to forget that he grew up "dirt poor" among the " 'masses' "; and the bookbinder Hussey, added in the revision, loses his daughter through malnutrition.

However, instead of joining efforts to elevate or fatten the masses, Herrick had been gauging, like Howard Sommers, the virtues of declining to fight clear of average mankind. A short story for the *Saturday Evening Post* of September 19, 1903—"Common Honesty"—portrayed a ruined businessman who erectly and cheerfully serves as a menial assistant to his old partner. Closer yet to the point of the new novel, "A Bull Market"—for the *Post* of January 27, 1900—glorified a wife who makes her husband confess his corruption from speculating in stocks and settle for a humbler scale of expenses.

In *The Common Lot*, the very wifely Helen Hart delivers the basic rationale for its plot: "We are bound to one another inseparably in this life of ours; we make a society that is a composite. Whatever we may do to weaken the sense of that common bond disintegrates society. Whatever we can do to deepen the sense of that bond makes life stronger, better for all! " With the same socio-emotional tone Herrick amplifies that she "had in large measure that rare instinct for democracy, the love of being like others in joy and sorrow" (144).

The antithesis of the greedy matron, she disapproves as her husband gradually relaxes his standards as an architect and his private ethics for money to support his high-flying tastes. When long-indulged hopes of a huge legacy fall through, Jackson Hart escalates into collusion with a builder who cheats on materials; a mass tragedy caused by one of their shoddy façades plunges Hart into a wavering crisis, from which he emerges in penitent unanimity with his wife. In looking back, the reader feels that the denouement was all settled from the first page, if not from Herrick's Harvard days. But architecture and dishonest contractors were at least fitting subjects for the Chicago of the time.

Also befitting the time of Theodore Roosevelt and *Realpolitik*, Hart always finds a rationalization when his conscience rebels at the next step. But his wife—who is impervious to what Herrick styles "our good Americans of the 'strenuous' school," and disgusted by the moral losses of the scramble for success—demands that he do open penance and incur the danger of prosecution when an apartment hotel that he designed suddenly burns to the ground. The builder's cheating on the already thin plans was the critical factor, but the architect is made to watch the holocaust, at which his draftsman calls him a "son of a bitch"—spelled out, says a careful scholar, for the first time in American fiction.[5] His wife, too "austerely virtuous" in Herrick's hindsight, also demands that her husband return to the office from which he started his rise, that he go back "Into the Ranks," the title for the last section and the working one for the entire novel. Though Herrick later also had qualms about the human soundness of the ending, they were not present the time. In a subplot, Venetia Phillips, daughter of a widow who helps Hart make the wrong choices, renounces most of her fortune and marries the dedicated researcher.

Herrick had joined the nascent swell of doubts about the gospel of success, but with a confusing viewpoint. Forbidding retreat to Mexico or to a New England farm, Hart's wife insists on a subsidiary gospel that played into the hands of the robber barons; she exhorts: "There is work! the best thing in life,—work for itself, without pay in things, without bribes! " (372). More puzzling, the chastened Hart agrees to letting his children enter the "universal struggle no better equipped than with the possession of health and a modest education." But even saturnine Coburn does his pure research with an eye on gold medals; in other words, "work" as a prime value usually breeds desire for cash proof of its competence; and the battle to subsist, however healthy for character, often spurs an ambition to head the pack. Herrick did not foresee what has been learned from and beyond the Progressive movement: it is difficult to set an accepted ceiling for the profits of work and harder yet to allow only the right degree of competition. In 1904 the future hid unsuspected traps in craft unions and in antitrust laws. Besides, *The Common Lot* scanted the main issues by picking its case study from the professions.

Only slightly ahead of the mass media, Herrick had already pondered the array of professions that had sprung up as the captains of industry learned both to appreciate expertise and to pay well for it. Currently the public of the monthly magazines liked to read especially about architects, impressively useful because of the building boom in houses as well as factories and yet glamorous because of their esthetic side. In fact, an architect had lately shaped a too-expensive house for Herrick, leaving him with a smattering of technicalities and jangled nerves.

But *The Common Lot* finally intended to confront a more general type, the intellectual who, no longer attracted to the ministry, has to work in the secular world but wants a higher standard than profits. Gloomy despite its tone of uplift, *The Common Lot* decided that a professional man could earn sizable fees only by compromising on quality and integrity. Coburn perceived this about the practice of medicine before the novel opens; at his club, but before he is ready to comprehend, Hart hears the same view ably expounded (54—55). In *The Web of Life* Sommers had preached a semi-monastic code for the professions. Hart's selling out sets merely a warning example; Coburn, whose research eventually makes a splash in the medical journals, sets more of a positive model but has paid his own lean way. Neither man shows that a lawyer or engineer or architect can follow his ideals while staying in the good graces of the power elite.

Surprisingly, *The Common Lot* gave more concrete indications of how the masses might subsist with dignity; it did so from several sides, put in fair opposition. While dramatic propriety seldom raises questions for the analyst of Herrick's ideas, the reader of this novel must sometimes ponder who, if anybody, speaks for the author. At least not Judge Pemberton, who growls that the "one aim" of the lower classes is "to get somebody's money without working for it." Though the judge deserves respect for austerely exposing graft, touches of rhetoric make it clear that Herrick had moved away from the iron-fisted school of economics. Where he had moved to needs much closer scrutiny.

Another harsh view gets support from Coburn, who rose from the social floor through drive worthy of John D. Rockefeller. He belittles charity workers, particularly the "settlement cranks"—though Lovett had begun his frequent cross-town trips to Hull House—and argues that "you can't really know anything about folks until you earn your bread as they do, because you have to or starve." So far, this view could stem from Leo Tolstoy, whose neo-primitive social criticism Herrick was reading. But Tolstoy would have mournfully scorned Coburn's remedy: "What men need is a chance to help themselves at the pot. And the only way they'll ever get that is to fight for it. Fight the hoggish ones who want the whole loaf" (138). This harshness gains dignity because Coburn is at the moment capably treating a mangled dog, but the situation turns ironic as he goes on: "The real fact is, most of the world isn't worth the bother of saving it from its fate. They are refuse junk." Asked why he labors bleary-eyed at medical research, he lamely rejoins that he wants to impress the wealthy physicians who sneer at him.

A sharply opposing view comes from pale, slender Hussey, too awkwardly inserted after the serial version ran in the *Atlantic Monthly*. Trapped on the bottom rung, though a craftsman with creative talents, he calls for a wiser scale of rewards and, therefore, a new system of economics. Too bitter to mourn over a wife and daughter strangled by poverty, he "assumed calmly that the present state of society was wasteful and unjust, and that already, here and there, men and women were beginning to wake from the individualistic nightmare and were ready to try an altogether new manner of living together" (215). While avoiding the label, he can only have some form of socialism in mind, one more thoughtful and constructive than that of his fellow bookbinder in James's *Princess Casamassima*. Also, he is easily more believable as a personality than James's Hyacinth Robinson, who could not subvert a lemonade stand.

Helen Hart, the moral paragon of the novel, learns to rebel almost as far as Hussey, concluding: "Surely a new order of the world was to be born, wherein the glory of life should not be for the ferocious self-seekers, wherein all that was fine in man should not be tainted with greed! " (231). A few months after *The Common Lot* had hard covers, Herrick wrote uneasily to Lovett, who was composing novels long since ignored: "You and I are both too much inclined to poke in a kind of semi-socialistic motif that has nothing to do with the story." His qualms were justified on grounds of political clarity rather than structure, for Helen Hart's one specific plank can not qualify as even quasi-socialism. Her support of education for the working class goes toward "industrial institutes," which will teach useful skills but omit those that might stir ambitions to become "department managers or proprietors." Rather than greater income or power for the masses, she advocates a "little more sanity," unwittingly drifting toward the platform that had led the Federalist and Whig parties to extinction at the polls.

Looked at coldly, *The Common Lot* asked for little change beyond helping the masses find a wiser contentment. Herrick could not embrace any party implying that environment is stronger than conscience. Helen's moral rigidity does soften to pity for those who fall under the lure of rampant materialism; unlike Jack Pemberton, she finally concedes that she has demanded inhuman heroics from the free will.[6] Yet the Chicago that "deadened" Hart's sense of beauty had less potency as an evil force than it had had in *The Web of Life*. *The Common Lot* took root from the hope of spiritual rebirth, of a regeneration cast in religious terms except for chary mention of God. While judging it the "best of all Herrick's novels," Oscar Cargill sums it up as a "quaint book which insists on the value of integrity and the cleansing power of the admission of guilt."[7] Springtime nature infuses Hart with the strength to turn away from "sin"; his personal Easter, as Herrick later called it, is all too typical of the conversion scenes that dominate American fiction until World War I. Herrick broke free of their tyranny only after the way out was well trodden.

Sentimentalists enjoy a conversion scene best when a male plays it, after being inspired by a female. Though Ibsen's ubiquitous hand lay behind Helen's walking out on her yet unregenerate husband, she sounded like the righteous wife of a thousand novels in the gaslight era. Her friendship with Venetia Phillips was therefore artfully incongruous, for that daring social-ite looked forward to the emancipated flappers of the Jazz Age. Berating the men of her set as "damn dull" outside the office, she argues that their women, excluded from the downtown fight for dollars, become "sports" out of boredom; she lets pursuers kiss her merely to see what they will do next and reports that they go "back to the ape mighty quick" (201–5). In her most jaded mood she wishes to "have the kids without the husband." Her raciness abraded reviewers except the one for *Club Fellow* who appropriately held that she "made the book worthwhile." At least, as a moral realist, she convincingly stirs fresh air into every episode that she can.

Several lesser characters radiate the same vitality. Graves, the slippery contractor, and Everett Wheeler, a laconic and cynical yet decent lawyer, never waver away from credibility or toward rebirth. Venetia's mother, perfumed and ambitious, reminds one critic of Strindberg's monsters in velvet. Powers Jackson, with whose funeral the novel opens, keeps emerging in retrospect as a believable mixture of qualities. However, Jackson Hart, the crucial case, seldom acts like more than a device and eventually compounds this failure by drawing on inner resources not hinted at before. On other counts also, Herrick fumbled the common problem of making the ending as persuasive as the beginning. The first chapter, which contrasts the funeral sermon and the thoughts of the apparent mourners, is striking. Also handled well are Hart's fling in a dive near the stockyards and suburban flashes catching the gradations between Eversley Heights and Popover Plains. But even Coburn and Venetia sag into a syrupy wedding scene, its quality accented by the limping dog that first brought them together.

The Common Lot belabored Hart as a highly imitative designer. Yet its own technique showed no originality or boldness. Furthermore, it showed faults that were becoming habits: a shower of coincidences, frequent sentences of commentary driven in with exclamation points, an attempt to get weightiness by hurrying over a long time span. This last flaw sprang from misapplying Herrick's classroom dictum, then sound in view of current practice: "Novels that present characters & *develope* them, showing growth, are greater than novels that present static character in event." As yet, he could not distinguish, or else achieve, the effect of distinguishing between growth and conversion. In time, his most credible men and women would be, ironically, strong personalities who stick to their grooves, impervious to rancor or defeat or—less often—flattery.

V *A Peak of Achievement*

The next novel, his best known and most highly praised, conspicuously lacks a conversion scene; instead *The Memoirs of an American Citizen* (1905) builds up several standard opportunities for Edward Van Harrington to repent his hard-knuckled dealing and then lets him ignore or spurn them. Likewise, Herrick of the *Memoirs* makes his march upward in the business world suprisingly free of surprises, reverses, or sacrifices to conventional plot once he gets his footing in big-city ways. This frustration of tearful clichés also holds for the supporting cast, especially Jane Dround, another likely carrier of melodrama. She rings quietly true as a vicarious tycoon, combative yet poised, keen to hear about Harrington's forays yet gentle in coddling her weak husband. When Harrington does record some intimate exchanges with her, he concedes that adults seldom talk so openly; his palely genteel wife, whom he married for love and treats kindly, lets their conflicts subside into a tacit truce. In his jousts with other meatpackers, his bluff mind brushes aside what little eloquence he hears. To reverse the analysis, the terseness of his "memoirs" fits both his private character and social type very firmly, achieving—said one critic—a "beauty of consistency that reminds one of modern iron constructions."

Much of the excellence in the *Memoirs* rises, therefore, from working through Harrington as the first-person narrator, used here for the only time in a Herrick novel though his teaching notes long showed awareness of the possibilities. Never far out of favor, even with Henry James despite his grumblings, the "I" narrator had become popular of late through supposedly nonfictional "confessions." As the *Memoirs* were being shaped, David Graham Phillips—more talented than painstaking as a novelist, more interested in muckraking than in technique—published *The Master-Rogue*, ostensibly by a robber baron who convicts himself much more clumsily than Harrington. More broadly, Herrick may have intended to emulate the Greville memoirs, printed a few years before, by domesticating the inside account of rivalry and intrigue at the royal courts of Europe. Business and politics aside, with the *Memoirs* Herrick joined the surprising number of American novelists who have reached their peak through the "I" narrator.

For Herrick, this device, whatever circuits it opened for the national psyche, helped to attain the understated "objectivity" he still aimed at sometimes. Projecting first a picaresque framework, he realized that any overt judgment would blunt the comedy that was vital to the genre and also that a business magnate hardly wears the hat of a rogue-outcast. Or he may merely have decided, reacting as usual against his previous novel, to block any temptation to moralize. Or, simply and positively, he may have made that rare intuitive leap that brings subject, technique, the writer's unique talents, and his weaknesses into the most effective collocation. In any case, Harrington was fortunately allowed to tell his story on his own grounds, fairly confident of convincing his readers. Though Mark Twain reversed the moral poles, with his narrator deeming himself in the wrong, *Adventures of Huckleberry Finn* is a shining example of judgment by implication. Better matching, though artless, examples are the interviews that self-made tycoons were granting as solemnly as Silas Lapham gives the first overview of his character. The words "American Citizen" in Herrick's title turn out to have been understatement, of course. Harrington rises to the top plateau of finance before buying a seat in the United States Senate—a "millionaires' club," some charged.

Herrick observed that the "real kernel of the story, its artistic truth," lay in Harrington's not being the "sort of man ever to know the whole truth about himself and life." Besides technique Herrick meant that any sizable degree of self-awareness would have aborted Harrington's rise. His drive springs partly out of vague frustration (he is a kind of nonacademic "dropout"). Exiled from a tiny Indiana town because of prankish restlessness, he drifts to Chicago, where he is quickly duped into worse trouble. When he does get a foot on the status ladder, he knows only that rising is better than falling; his natural combativeness makes him turn each step into a wider but more vulnerable perch in the packing-house industry. Too busy fighting to worry about improving the rules, he is puzzled when the muckrakers focus on him; and he protests that satisfying their ethics would have left him mired in poverty—rags-to-riches capitalists have never understood the dangers of wholeheartedly applying the gospel of success. At the end of the *Memoirs*, when his elevation to the Senate is clouded by abusive editorials, Harrington can only wonder: "Surely there was another scale, a grander one, and by this I should not be found wholly wanting! " (346).

Herrick avoided the reformer's mistake, however, of seeing the capitalist simplistically. Groping at times—"carefully unguarded," Howells said aptly—for a rationale, Harrington leans toward feeling—in Howells' words, again—that he is the "agent, the ally, not to say the accomplice, the 'pal' of Providence."[8] Yet this chord, so prevalent among the first millionaires, is struck seldom. Likewise, though Harrington can invoke the "survival-of-the-fittest" doctrine if forced to and can claim superior adaptation to its economic form, he takes pride in not acting rapacious. His most common defense holds, "I was made for just this earth, good and bad as it is,—and I must go my way to my end" (218). In other words, intent on pragmatic fulfillment, he is merely following his needs in the arena that destiny allotted him. Partly in apology, Herrick later observed that Harrington is left with a nagging "sense of the incompleteness of his triumph after all." But the reader has full reason to expect that Harrington will play national politics to the hilt; if less blithely, he will do so just as aggressively as when he bested the stockyard giants. Typical of the American self-sentenced for life to the competitive battle, he finds every victory incomplete after a while and raises his sights.

In passing, F. O. Matthiessen has suggested that making a tycoon his narrator forced Herrick to intimate his own attitudes too heavily. But the wonder is that he exerted so much restraint, which confused several reviewers: the Chicago *Tribune* accepted the *Memoirs* as "sympathetic satire," and the Chicago *Record-Herald* cautiously decided that it "reads more like a justification than anything else." Certainly Herrick, rewriting more than usual, fought to achieve balance. His changes after the serial version in the *Saturday Evening Post* improved Harrington's inner logic and perhaps his likability; the book-version Harrington displays courage, magnanimity, open-handedness, and loyalty to his friends and refuses almost quixotically to join forces with a dangerously powerful but arrogant Jewish banker. (A wavering vein of anti-Semitism runs through Herrick's work before 1920.) Even more than most of us, Herrick, who later frankly relished his despotism in the Virgin Islands, admired the individualist who masters events and accidents. Vicarious delight shines through Harrington's financial coups. In a more deliberate touch, the outside world usually judges him too harshly, impelling the fair-hearted reader to feel sympathetic.

This last touch has led some recent critics to overstate still Herrick's approval of his businessman, to assert that they are kindred souls. In fact,

Herrick, who played the stock market and rated himself a deft hand with money, liked to claim that his sureness with the mind and affairs of Harrington came from inner projection instead of close models. However, he was drawing on the career of the late Philip D. Armour; this packing-house magnate had earlier supplied some features of the industrialist in *The Common Lot* who founds a technical institute. More vitally, Herrick distinguished between, to phrase it as simply as his view deserves, good and bad capitalists. This distinction is evident in his previous novels as well as in "Common Honesty," a story published while the *Memoirs* was in first draft; the story implies that it deals with an exception in flaying a hardware merchant—his specialty is "nails"—who swindles his kindly partner. When Herrick wrote a series of unsigned editorials for the *Saturday Evening Post* in 1906, one praised Marshall Field while another attacked John D. Rockefeller, predicting that Americans "never will admire him, never will respect him."

Those eager to condemn Harrington as a robber-baron can quote chapter and line. Inconsistent with his blunt and decisive ways, he is made to tolerate the chiding of too many friends and dependents—his brother, wife, sister-in-law, minister, first employer in the packing-house district, and even his attorney. At his darkest hour he is spurned by a righteous New England banker who, it is implied, invests only in immaculate ways—a convincing position perhaps to the muckrakers who were waxing indignant because they believed in such alternatives. Yet the *Memoirs* failed to show an option that worked for any of a dozen minor characters who cross-section the business world. The difficulty in fixing a moral scale must lead to the conclusion that Herrick's attitude was intricately, persuasively balanced. Crucially, Harrington inherits a naiveté about the social effects of his type. To a disturbing degree he "is American society itself. He is corrupt, but he hardly realizes it and when he does he cannot act on his self-knowledge. Those who follow him are helped materially but lose their moral innocence, while those that don't are the obscure and impotent."[9] To reject him totally is to reject the latter-day New World.

If results to the present are proof, any setting should be sharply local if it hopes to typify American society. The *Memoirs*, the last of Herrick's novels taking place mainly in Chicago, except for the autobiographical *Chimes*, succeeded best in etching both Midwestern and national patterns. Not paradoxically it did so partly because the succinct narrator wasted few words toward that end, depending on vivid glimpses such as the passage in which a Yankee exile waves his arm at the South Side and bitterly asks why anybody would settle there except to make money (52). The packing house is a pungently distinctive microcosm for the business arena; and the

Haymarket trial, at which Harrington serves on the jury, distinctively draws in the proletarians. In total weight, the lower classes are neglected; and the bearded "anarchist" who assaults Harrington smells of grease paint; but an honest, even touching vignette of the cheap boarding houses could have pleased John Sloan during his phase as an "Ash-can" painter. For once, despite Floyd Dell's opinion, Herrick made Chicago seem a place rather than a "problem."

The drive and depth of the *Memoirs* have impressed sensitive critics. Better than some heavily documented novels, it raises concreteness into wide implications; a Danish critic saw Harrington as the New World apogee of the Napoleonic type. The *Memoirs* gives more while demanding more of the reader than any other American novel of the decade except *Sister Carrie*. Herrick understated his case when he confided to Lovett in 1905: ". . . without a great deal of conceit, I can comfort myself that at least there's nothing much better going among my contemporaries."[10] And perhaps Howells was not overstating, as he often did in kindness, when he said the next year: "You have asked . . . too much of our generation, but it is high and brave in you to have asked it."[11] At this point, Herrick struck many as the leading novelist of that generation, with shining heights ahead. The *Memoirs* had a Danish translation in 1907, as did *The Real World* in 1912.

Ominously, *The Memoirs of an American Citizen* still showed many of Herrick's faults. But they were much less noticeable and, his admirers could hope, less entrenched. Pausing for breath, Herrick resolved, after surveying the quality and quantity of his fiction, that the next step must be truly major—with, say, the scope of *The Web of Life*, the aspiration of *The Real World*, the wide sympathy of *The Common Lot*, and the sure-handedness of the *Memoirs*. He would labor to make that step. The result, after three years, was surprising in almost every way.

CHAPTER 3

The Crisis of Intentions

I *Return to the Short Story*

Still a few years short of the age of forty, Herrick had sound reasons for self-confidence by 1905: he had already attained some mature fiction; indeed, a few critics later judged that he had already published his best work. His promotion that year to a full professorship at the University of Chicago—with generous provision for leaves and part-time schedules— assured security in a second, more predictable career. With *The Memoirs of an American Citizen*, he had conquered the Realist's enervating fear of exhausting the subjects he can treat authentically. Success in creating his meatpackers made Herrick "feel free boldly to handle whatever stuff attracted my imagination . . . by penetrating by the inner eye into other conditions of life removed from mine own." From study of the great novelists, he knew that their "inner eye" had easily outstripped the physical sight; now he believed that his could too and that he could hold his prolific pace. Actually, he was too prolific, almost matching the journalistic dash of Jack London and David Graham Phillips—when he should have been steeping in his material like Dreiser.

Yet few novelists deliberatively slow down for the sake of quality, as literary critics would prefer. Besides, Herrick, despite his praise of asceticism, kept spending beyond his income; and, despite his preachments about laboring like the multitude, he was continually taking leave from even his half-time salary. In 1906 he therefore hacked out a series of unsigned editorials for the *Saturday Evening Post*, commenting shrewdly but raggedly on a wide range of topics.[1] But he wasted this income and more energy by traveling almost pointlessly. From the first, overreacting against the dangers of seclusion, he had fretted about the need to "immerse himself in the swift stream of life" and follow an outgoing pattern. He never found—and could not have—a pattern that satisfied both his fastidiousness and his suspicion of intellectuals. He periodically tried Europe but more and more thought it as "vulgar" as America since he shunned artistic coteries. It never struck him that the avant-garde might offer more than his search for "any bit of experience" outside his two "cloistered" professions or that deep-diving insight would help his art better than pellmell "contacts with reality."

Most patently, Herrick lacked a deeper, richer conception of the short story. Defining it negatively, as a genre incapable of tracing the growth of character achieved in the best novels, he gave no sign of exploiting its brevity as a unique challenge. Instead, his short stories too often used changeable personalities, after all, and read like synopses for triple-deckers; his stories of the mid-1890's remained more interesting as a group both in theme and technique. In self-defense, he regarded himself more and more as solely a novelist; and he softened the sting of failure by pointing out that the editors of the magazines that paid big money shied away from the profound or experimental: such magazines had become "huge advertising billboards" without the elevated and elevating goals of the *Atlantic Monthly* in its greatest days during his boyhood. But the cluster of stories that he published in 1907 and 1908 mostly catered to this new market.

Fittingly, the best of them did appear in the *Atlantic* for March, 1908. "The Temple of Juno," about a chance meeting in a Mediterranean byway between a couple estranged ten years before, depends on subtlety as the husband gains a degree of accusatory self-insight while discovering that his wife has grown somewhat in the meantime; reconciliation is likely at the close, but even then Herrick depends on implication. At the other extreme of his marketing range was the weekly *Collier's*, which was stiffening its Gibson Girl froth with muckraking. Its issue of October 19, 1907, carried Herrick's worst story for these years, "Papa's Stratagem," a feeble copy of O. Henry's ingenious plotting. Though it has parallels with Herrick's better work, the only touch worth mention is the genial sympathy for a banker who wants to feel needed in Cleveland, Ohio, rather than to wander elegantly about Europe. Even this aspect reassured the *Collier's* audience that its view of human nature was sound.

On the whole, Herrick aimed higher; and *Scribner's Magazine* accepted most of his efforts, perhaps hoping to lure his novels away from Macmillan. Pretentious and melodramatic, his "Avalanche" for *Scribner's* of June, 1907, had a steel core in the wife who perceives that her mountain-climbing husband is courting death. More interesting, "The General Manager," in the issue of March, 1908, grew out of Herrick's dislike for literary salons. Its title applied to a young widow who toys with promoting young writers; by giving up on an aspirant who has fallen in love with her, she drives him to succeed but also to outgrow her intellectually. This story, allowing no Shelleyean heroics to writers, managed the ironies more delicately than the new century had as yet learned to like. Typical of the crude irony dictated by current taste was "The Master of the Inn," published in *Scribner's* for December, 1907; indeed, it suited so well that its reissue as a wide-margined novelette called for at least eighteen printings. It also stirred up a stream of urgent mail from readers wanting treatments from the model for its master healer.

As a matter of fact, there was one. In the spring of 1907, Herrick, caught in a multiheaded crisis, had a mild breakdown. While harassed by deepening conflicts with his wife, he had been laboring over his next novel, a "Colossus of Matrimony," which was scaled more grandly than anything before it. Body and nerves rebelled against years of overstrain; his digestion faltered, and long spells of insomnia haunted his nights. Someone recommended a Doctor John G. Gehring, whose snug sanitarium in the Maine mountains sold country air and exercise, a simple diet, spiritual uplift, and a few drugs. A hypochondriac who wasted the time of too many clinics, Herrick underwent Gehring's treatment in the summer of 1907. It gave him "peace" with a warm touch that reminded him of the old family doctor. For *Scribner's* of January, 1908, his story "In the Doctor's Office" belabored a brisk diagnostician for making impersonal tests and charts on a patient who is simply pining away for her estranged husband.

In "The Master of the Inn," the healer of psychosomatic ills obviously resembles Gehring; but Herrick later pointed out that Gehring, unlike the fabulous "Master," prescribed drugs and accepted patients of both sexes. Because more justly suspect than most, Herrick writhed under any accusations of crudely or cruelly transferring biography to his fiction. He once rejoined soundly that such charges often strain for proof while ignoring obvious differences. Probing deeper, and making this story a test case, he warned of the "transformation by opposites ... the idealization process that often springs paradoxically enough from a disenchanting experience."[2] Though the principle is valid, reality was more tangled: Gehring had private assurances he was the admired model; on the other hand, the Master gives the effect of a wistful fantasy or feverish ideal.

In a boldly eloquent style, with biblical undertones, "The Master of the Inn" deifies a selfless healer, who is called Father by the jaded surgeons, lawyers, and architects who seek his monastic refuge to be put back in functioning order. Though Gehring, according to Herrick, dispensed "the Holy Grail and Cathartics—equally mixed," the Master relies on the "Holy Ghost and Sweat—with a good bath afterward! " Minimizing theory, he eases tensions through outdoor work, revives the zest of bodily fitness, and elicits at the crucial moment a "confession." The cleansed and recouped patient marches away as a disciple, bearing the Secret: an uncomplicated faith in Man and Life and Soul, in forgetting pain through work, in Labor not "merely for oneself; but also something for others." At the climax, built on another of Herrick's leaden coincidences, the Master shows a superhuman ability to forgive injury. In his total effect, he proves that Herrick's desertion from organized religion had still left him a "man of piety," one deeply swayed by Christian symbols as well as by the concepts of soul and salvation, which continued to guide the "kind of questions he asks about the human condition and the very terms in which he asks them."[3]

Because it spoke so elliptically, "The Master of the Inn" could be welcomed by several active movements: the old religion of humanity, the rising interest in psychiatry, the health faddism always current, the "ethical culture" group, and especially the mind-over-matter school swelled by the Christian Scientists.[4] In 1909, William Vaughn Moody, a friend and faculty colleague, published a play *The Faith Healer*, in which a mystic from the spacious Southwest confounds a physician and a Darwinist skeptic; Herrick's latent Christianity had kept him just as open-minded about "higher" levels of mind than science usually recognizes. Furthermore, his emotional crisis had left an interest in psychic tensions that can disrupt the realm of matter. From one perspective, "The Master of the Inn" did blame them on the drive for success; but Herrick could not allow environment such ultimate victory, as his next novel, *Together*, showed. It ended with a medico-religious figure who, even more than the Master, radiates a faith by which to live in, rather than retreat from, society; and its message suggests that Herrick's crisis was partly ideological, not just somatic.

II *A "Colossus of Matrimony"*

This crisis is underscored by the near confusion at many points of *Together* (1908). Almost four years of ambitiously reshuffling its plan left telltale marks on its ideas. "Originally conceived"—says the most competent student of Herrick[5]—to display the "effects of individualism in modern marriage," it eventually groped in more directions than it could manage—a disarray intensified by a crisis in technique and by the signs of even deeper malaise. A few years later, Herrick, more in pride than apology, declared that *Together* "grew more blindly and more unconsciously than any other book I ever wrote." But it grew under a plethora of synopses, statements of purpose, and experiments in method as he wrestled with a plot that could delineate the marriages of several contrasting couples—an idea fresh at the time.

Goaded by failure to attain the pitch of Romantic intensity he dreamed of, Herrick had decided on an impetuous tone. Unfortunately, this meant an even less responsible style than before—one also made loose on the theory that, since fiction succeeds primarily through the vitality of its vision, concern with the envelope of words can be inhibiting. Or, from the reader's viewpoint, Herrick felt simply that manner, if too polished, detracts from matter. Even years afterward, having returned to greater care with rhetoric, Herrick insisted that the "most widely influential imaginative writers of the past . . . were always more concerned with the substance of what they were doing than with manner or form."[6] In *Together* the style often proved slovenly; aiming at urgency, it only suggests haste. Incidentally, he had begun to compose on a typewriter, which seemed to encourage his tendency toward adding a second or third sentence when the first one needed refining.

The positive aspect of scorning involuted finish was a decision to strive for epic breadth. Fearing that his novels so far were cramped, he set out to enlarge their conventional length and "single character" frame. Lecturing in 1908 on "The Technique of the Novel," he deplored a trend toward "simplification" or "smaller canvases" because "it limits the creator in a form that is peculiarly adapted to the presentation of life broadly . . . the wide expanse, the maze of life where multitudinous forces act and interact." Though the ambitious mood had contracted by 1915, his first sustained effort at self-assessment observed that *Together* had shaken off Maupassant's admonition "to present character as objectively as possible, to show men and women from the outside and to guess at their souls." Obviously, Herrick had hoped to outdo his preceding work, although, as a fatal sign, he did not claim that his theme demanded magnitude and complexity of form. Even so, a prominent reviewer for the prominent *Bookman* (August, 1908) found in *Together* the "breadth, the sweeping generality of Tolstoi's *Kreutzer Sonata* and Zola's *Fécondité*."

Another review (in the *Forum*) gave Zola sole credit for the "panoramic . . . wide sweep of the picture, the impression of urgent, thronging life, the effect of many-sidedness." In his lectures Herrick often named Fielding, Balzac, Thackeray, and Dostoevsky as models for a "freer, more epic" sweep undistracted by "exclusions," "refinements," or "subtleties." Still, the comparison with Tolstoy, whom he had rediscovered in 1905, doubtlessly pleased him best. While he now argued that almost every great novelist reveals his values, Tolstoy had done so majestically. Likewise, Herrick now believed firmly—and wistfully—that major fiction exudes its creator's personality, as Tolstoy's surely did. On other counts, as he summed them up, Tolstoy "alone of all the moderns had the full sense of the epic character of the novel, with its complexity of characters and interests, its large fluid unity." This effect of fluid unity was the most beguiling of all. Herrick jotted in 1908: "Looseness of form in Tolstoi—

really the most subtle realization of Life because Life does not present any artificial Unity. . . ." Covetous of the Russian's touch for achieving both grandiosity and rich detail, yet of keeping the effect of an open universe, the American learned too late that looseness in itself works no such wonders.

As a corollary to his ambition for a "more epic" form, Herrick decided that any enduring work of fiction must succeed as "social history." Happily, this decision led to a firmer play between the individual and his milieu and between humdrum routine and historic events. *The Web of Life* depicted both the surfaces of Chicago and its upheavals, but the strong-willed hero made them seem too ephemeral. In *Together*, respect for how strongly the milieu may pull on even the spiritually erect gave much more density to the homes, clothing, games, and occupations of humanity. Also, a deeper grasp of society eased the temptation to seek weight through riots or wars, which Herrick now saw as peaks in a chain rather than as unique accidents.

In *The Web of Life*, Sommers takes part in famous events of his era, yet seems detached from the mainstream. *Together* seldom probes beyond Isabelle Lane's clique, yet often makes the reader feel that the early twentieth century is at his fingertips. The underlying view of man as a node of relations spun by his time and place partly carried over into the next novel—and soon after that into notes for a magnum opus that was to be "no less than a survey of American life from 1870 to 1910, to be encompassed in three volumes chronicling the history of three generations of a New England family that migrates west after the Civil War, realizes a fortune from the opportunities created by the Chicago Fire, and founds a dynasty that holds sway throughout the troubled years of industrial growth preceding the first World War."[7] Since Herrick never fleshed out this prospectus for a New World Galsworthy, *Together* came nearest to fulfilling his ideal of the novelist as historian.

In the United States, more than anywhere else, social history intertwines with getting and spending. Therefore, the dimension of the past was added to *Together* by contrasting present ways of prospering with those of a Colonel Price, a native of New England and a field officer during the Civil War, who migrated to the Midwest where, "with the plainest personal habits and tastes, taking no tarnish from luxury . . . seeing things larger than dollars," he and his kind "made the best aristocracy that this country has seen. Their coat of arms bore the legend: Integrity and Enterprise" (111). Proud of being "traders" and "merchants" (the Colonel sells basic hardware), they avoided speculation as sin, gave fair value, created profit rather than draining it from the flesh of the multitude, and did more than any other group to "develop and civilize" the country. In short, so simplistically as to approach parody, Colonel Price embodied the Whig or Liberal version of history; and he was a more suitable creation for chastening the House of Lords than the banking house of Morgan. Given too bald a name in *Together*, he had already been idealized as Colonel Hitchcock in *The Web of Life*.

But John Lane, Price's son-in-law and main foil, was handled realistically. Herrick's shrewd essay "The American Novel," published in the *Yale Review* for April, 1914, later charged that our writers had failed to seize the "one big theme of the past twenty years—the story of the money-maker, his inner meaning and his self-explanation." Helped by his wife's prestige, Lane rises from junior executive to the managerial elite of railroading while profiting from inside tips on the stock market. He falls short of Edward Van Harrington's stature also because he is not made fiercer nor more ambitious than his associates. For these very reasons, on the other hand, he is thoroughly convincing. Better than Harrington, furthermore, he reveals a clearly twentieth-century style of business as it merged with intricate finance, controlled by boards of well-connected diplomats rather than by the lone wolf and counting on expert flouting of the law. If Herrick had cared to make this vein central, he might have matched the solidity of Dreiser's Frank Cowperwood at work.

Except for lapses, Herrick wisely made Lane taciturn, as disinclined to abstract "self-explanation" as Mark Hanna. Instead, with ironic asides on Social Darwinism, *Together* demonstrated how a railroad could strangle a small coal operator who was given no chance to prove his competitive fitness; and at a fancy dinner party, a cynic described how runty pigs result from a sow with eight shoats but only six teats, just as on the human level "there are a thousand mouths to every teat, and a few big, fat fellows are getting all the food" (88, 196–97). The turns of plot often implied that talk is mostly obfuscatory, like the eloquence of corporation lawyers who outshine the second-raters that the state can afford, or useless, like the plaints of the reformers who were shaping up the Progressive movement. The reformers did not expect sneers from Herrick, who thought in moral terms as strongly as they did. But perhaps with the help of Lovett, who kept moving to the Left, Herrick had concluded that political issues only mask the economic pressures.

The action of *Together* followed such an analysis in Lane's career and that of Percy Woodyard, a high-minded crusader used as a lightning rod by the financiers and their statesmen. Repelled by the jingoism of the Spanish-American War, Herrick had distrusted Theodore Roosevelt from the start. In the jaded light of the 1920's he charged that a "sounder conservative" never graced the White House than Roosevelt, whose reforms only made capitalism run all the merrier, and that the Progressive party had never proposed "one fundamental or radical change, political or economic." In *Together*, Isabelle Lane, with her final insight, asserted that Roosevelt and all the "good element" were not opposing the "spirit of conquest" but merely asking the fighters to go by the "rules of the game" (542). As both passing and basic touches in the novel prove, Herrick, like every sincere citizen, had been shocked by the revelations of the muckrakers. But, like Lincoln Steffens, he had probed beneath the hullabaloo of the muckraking publications.

Herrick even accused a fictitious *People's Magazine* and its flag-waving impresario, who resembled S. S. McClure, of turning a quick profit on such exposés but of continuously defending the status quo. Then, betraying the indecision that sapped the ending, *Together* declaimed that laws for factory inspection, a shorter work week, or less child labor would not "right the wrong of life in any deep sense" (523–24). As to what would, Herrick warned like a latter-day transcendentalist: "Each must start with self and right that. . . . Yes, the world needed a Religion, not movements nor reform! " But the accumulating texture of the novel had made outside pressures seem solid and powerful; they demanded more than a prescription for self-reform. Issued by Isabelle Lane, this pronouncement offered little help to runty weaklings or to the small operator swallowed by a trust, no matter if it held the last hope for rescuing her from the narcissism her upper-class ease had bred.

This imbalance of economic criticism and remedy could slip in because the primary emphasis of *Together* was intended for remedying the flaws of modern marriage. Herrick later denied treating "problems" in his fiction, meaning that he aspired to more richness and depth than journalistic crusaders like Upton Sinclair. Still, he put an array of couples under a narrowed scrutiny, heralded by the title and an essay in the closing pages that was conceived as the opening chapter (513–18). Loftily ignoring his own fireside troubles, the essay held up an ideal, reached by the westering pioneers, of marriage as a partnership in practical goals and protested that, among the middle and upper classes, it had sagged into a sterile polarity in which the husband pursued game on Wall Street or its branches while the wife declined from a "comrade" into a pampered "spender." The main plot of *Together* featured Isabelle Lane, an heiress whose husband also makes good. She reluctantly bears one child, toys with empty diversions, graduates to always richer yet duller homes, and drifts toward adultery.

Her husband sins, to be sure, by dedicating his best energies to business. However, though Herrick usually stressed the male world like most novelists, wives are the center of attention here. In *Intellectual America* (1941) Oscar Cargill claims that the "themes of marital unhappiness, of the dominant woman, and of the clash of the sexes in the later Dreiser, Ben Hecht, Anderson, and even in the *Spoon River Anthology* derive probably" from Herrick. This assessment pushes truth into overstatement; no single mind or book, here or abroad, dominated the theme of the New Woman. In the same year as *Together*, David Graham Phillips, who amplified it harshly with *Old Wives for New*, muckraked the stylish matron as if she were a cartel. Most interesting among the many other novels was H. G. Wells's *Marriage* (1912), which was surprisingly close to much of Herrick's viewpoint at this period.

Still the backbone of the audience for fiction, women monitored it imperiously. Some raised so loud a hubbub about an insulting or immoral portrait in *Together* as to give it fast-selling notoriety. They obviously preferred soft reverence or, at worst, Howells' kindly satire. Herrick was trying to see them afresh, even wondering if some had traits, good and bad, that were traditionally masculine. More disturbingly, he was wondering if they were not tortuously shaped by their biology, the premise of Otto Weininger's cranky *Sex and Character*, which was praised by the most reflective wife in *Together*—though Herrick's *Chimes* later gibed at it. Yet, on the conscious level anyway, no war on women showed its hand or its obvious disguises in *Together*. In 1915, Herrick staunchly insisted that his fiction had been, indeed, often partisan to the supposed enemy. He might have added that the New Woman attacked in Isabelle was defended in vibrant Margaret Pole, heroine of what became the most discussed subplot.

This balancing went unnoticed because he chose to exemplify Margaret's depth and strength by letting her spend two ecstatic days with her lover, then calmly return to her silly husband. The flouting of Victorian morality ventured in *The Web of Life* had grown bolder in *Together*. In 1906, Herrick drafted a play in which the wife of an architect pushes her husband into the arms of another married woman who appreciates his esthetic side; when the philanderers, "having had their full love," perceive that the "best part of it is the soul," the architect and his wife amicably resume their family routine. Though Herrick was not prodigal like Mark Twain, who eased his bile with manuscripts ineligible for print, he hardly could have expected to get this play produced. The idyllic truancy in *Together* aroused a storm, and a reviewer signing himself from the University of the South raged about "phallic" and "Hindoo muck."[8] After extracting a private (but equivocal) denial of moral laxity, Howells produced a gingerly critique that fell back on the novel's "pathological decency." Not so judicious, some libraries and the Canadian post office declared the novel to be beyond the pale.

Together had overplayed its hand in several ways. To avoid the effect of mere impulse, it spun the adultery into almost major size; Margaret's lover must first help her carry the burden of a crippled son, for example. Enmeshed in a philosophizing about love that lasted another ten years, Herrick analyzed their two-day idyll with excruciating fineness; and, with the notion of lulling the straitlaced, he exalted his tone to where Margaret and her soul mate could not be ignored. Ironically, they drew fire away from the more shocking entente between Percy and Conny Woodyard, who agree before their marriage that either is to remain free for romantic liaisons. The public also ignored that Margaret next puts physical love aside forever in order to prove that the spirit had moved her instead of the flesh. Reluctant to admit failure with this masochistic twist, Herrick tried to believe that the furor began from dismay at the cool reactions credited to Isabelle during her bridal night. Doing so at least let him feel all the more contemptuous toward prudery.

The hubbub over Margaret's code of love hid the fact that it invoked a broader value, altruism, most dramatically expressed by Vickers Price, Isabelle's once erring brother. In a scene that became for Herrick the fulcrum of the action, Vickers provoked his own murder to save his sister from adultery. On a calmer level, Alice and Steve Johnston display a marriage based on loyalty and generosity, one ended only by his death while rescuing a stranger. Unshaken, Alice helps Isabelle see the "cheapness of her old ideals of freedom, intellectual development, self-satisfaction, that cult of the ego" (587). The heroine of *The Gospel of Freedom* gathered this knowledge from experience, but Isabelle has to be schooled by a faith-healer, a Dr. Renault who warns that "egotism is the pestilence of our day" (497, 499). He is also the source of her conclusion that mankind needs a "new religion," which he urges passionately though vaguely. Its most specific effect on his converts' practice is a resolve not to bring suffering down on others and to give wholehearted support in a crisis. Isabelle is converted just in time to stand by her husband when the railroad sacrifices him to the muckrakers.

Herrick would have resented the sneer that goes along with the label of faith-healer today. Dr. Renault radiates a godlike power and dignity, several magnitudes beyond the Master of the Inn. His country retreat even has fresher, sharper air; and he inspires Isabelle to seek the big sky of the Southwest. Positive thinking has convinced him that "Life is good—all of it—for every one" (468, 470) and, as corollary doctrines, that "life is plastic, human beings are plastic"; that a true self-reliance will elicit the "infinite in every moment of every life"; and that the "voice of the spirit" lurks everywhere (500–501). Many touches dignify these ideas since Herrick admired them, as his next two novels proved more piercingly if possible. His notebook for 1910–11 summed up "The New Morality" as spiritual courage, joy in life, and functioning vitality. Though it does not seem new to a student of Carlyle and Emerson, it borrowed zest from current iconoclasts like Nietzsche and William James, and it anticipated the ethics of the Chicago Renaissance.

By the scale of Herrick's fiction to date, *Together* showed the same mixture of old and new traits. Alice and Steve Johnston insist on sharing the common lot; Margaret Pole rises into the "real" world of purposive will; her husband is another weak dandy further corrupted in the stock market. Yet the characters, Herrick's widest array by far, are manipulated more gracefully and less obviously than his smaller casts. They drop in and out of sight naturally, with no final roll call; coincidence is, for once, almost negligible. More vitally, emulating Tolstoy's effect of universal sympathy, Herrick managed to curb his usually patent judgments. When last seen, some opportunists are going strong with no desire for Renault's services; others have won chastening insight and still face a hard road. The toughness and complexity of life remain to put Renault's optimism to endless test.

For a recent paperback edition of *Together*, Van Wyck Brooks ranked it the "best" of Herrick's novels. It does have authority, both in its probing of basic attitudes and in its re-creating of surfaces. Many scenes, as when Bessie and Rob Falkner grind toward their impasse over a scale of expenses or Conny Woodyard makes up her husband's mind again, ring as authentic to the core. By contrast, Margaret Pole's fortissimo range sins against taste. Normally, the taste of academics is bland yet consistent, as in Herrick's lesson plans; in shaking off blandness, he veered close to bombast unworthy of his opening panorama on Isabelle's wedding day and of the flexibly ironic tone of the first two hundred pages.

But the faults of *Together* are particularly irritating because of its own proof of how superior it could have been. Blake Nevius holds that it "was an important work of fiction beside which most American novels of the period seemed—and still seem—tame and undernourished." Any historical defense should add that in 1908 Herrick seemed the most imaginative novelist of his time, capable of a masterpiece. He thought so too as he immediately set to writing *A Life for a Life*.

III *Theories of Realism and Idealism*

His reputation, endorsed by the venerable Howells, had reached heights it would never top. Brimming with the vitalism projected into Renault, Herrick eyed fresh ranges of emotion. Sure that *Together* broke through to freer technique, he found the courage, for the only important time in his career, to think that the novel has no innate structure and that content may shape or even create method. Unhappily, this courage brought his deepest crisis as an artist. When *A Life for a Life*, his boldest effort, proved disastrous, he floundered desperately; this novel had led to disaster because it lacked a true set of coordinates. Though his lecturing and few book reviews toyed with basic terms, he never pursued them and often doubted they were worth pursuit. All in all, he was a Realist without an effectively supportive esthetic.

This lack was grounded in his New England upbringing and its precept that ethics makes the heart of any discourse and that genre is at best tangential. Herrick very seldom defended the charm or dignity of fiction as James, Edith Wharton, or almost any major creator of it did or will do. After teaching "contemporary" literature for twenty years, Herrick reported discussing it not "as aesthetics preponderatingly" but "as a kind of clinic of the modern spirit." His most thoughtful essay on the American novel (1914) argued that form, while of "absorbing importance" to the author, is "always secondary to the quality of his vision." Of course vision finally outweighs all devices; but Herrick too narrowly meant its ethical quality. Too often he judged his characters—how openly is not relevant— instead of sharing their predicaments. If he had tried better just to see experience before measuring it against what ought to be, he would have moved deeper into the ironic vision that informs most great Realism—and would have avoided the debacle of *A Life for A Life*.

But, blessed now with a wealth of sophisticated theory, we tend to ignore that Herrick was less fortunate. Compared with the French, our late-nineteenth-century Realists sadly lacked an indigenous, flourishing rationale. Furthermore, the Anglophilism rampant during Herrick's days at Harvard kept him from making a god of Howells or from even admiring John William DeForest. While turning to the European masters, whom Herrick still favored in the 1930's, he recoiled at any hint of decadence, esthetic or personal; the nauseating effects of "paresis" on Alves Preston's husband in *The Web of Life* had obvious parallels with Maupassant's notorious breakdown. And, once past the 1890's, Herrick seldom explored for fresh avant-gardes. For that matter, the early 1900's had few to offer close by, during an upsurge of historical romances. As Herrick fairly summarized in 1924, "Since Howells' strong earlier work, I consider that there has been little American fiction of good quality—Frank Norris, London, some of Phillips' books, two or three volumes by Mrs. Wharton. . . ."[9]

His French models, which cautiously included Flaubert's *Madame Bovary*, braced his strongest side—a belief that his duty as a novelist was to expose false conceptions and values. He could warn that "until we demand in our literature the same strong tonic of clear-sighted truth that we get from science, we shall remain morally flabby." Echoing what is virtually a convention of middleclass Realism and of Howells, episodes in his fiction scored the reading of novels that serve as mental or psychic escape. At least once Herrick went so far as to declare that one of his two master themes was the "eternal conflict between Illusion,—man's dream of the wonderful,—and reality." This conflict lay near the working heart of four of his underrated novels that were yet to come: *Clark's Field, One Woman's Life, Homely Lilla,* and—very late—*The End of Desire.* In a period when official dogmas hid, far more than usual, man's current motives and practices, any demand for baring the tawdry truth had therapeutic promise.

Very seldom, however, did Herrick follow the French in claiming for Realism the dignity and bite of scientific method; rather, if pressed for definitions, he invoked respect for the normal and common. With Howells, these terms sometimes implied a scientific typicality; but Herrick usually had in mind—citing Trollope—a low-keyed, warm rendering of humdrum surfaces or—as he remarked in *Together* (199)—a perspective in which the "most commonplace household . . . would be a wonderful cosmography."

Curiously, none of his novels approaches either kind of effect. Like James, he decried the taste for melodrama yet satisfied it much more often than not before World War I. Though Herrick vowed to let his characters work out their problems authentically and to have no fear of sounding dull, he kept drifting back toward a strongly plotted chain of events. He also drifted far from the intimately common or from Howells' democratic average.

His program for Realism cannot be fixed more closely than to say it "seems to insist only that the novelist will deal with the known, the actual, the contemporary, in such a way that the truth of his representation may be acknowledged by his audience."[10] Full-blown Naturalism was so foreign to Herrick's tastes that it posed neither an influence nor a threat. He could protest that Zola's work had more weight and skill than it was always granted, but it never appeared on his changing list of favorites. In Dreiser (who respected Herrick's writing), he saw, as late as 1931, primarily clumsiness and a "verbosity unparalleled in American letters"; his glimmerings of Dreiser's elemental honesty never steadied into appreciation. He silently passed over Stephen Crane's novels, though they were the antithesis of Dreiser's faults: Crane's personal habits were, rumor had it, decadent. Frank Norris, the last American Herrick might have turned to for a Naturalistic esthetics, churned about confusingly and, besides, clouded the issue with his special definitions.

The sad fact is that Herrick probed little beyond the great debate of the 1880's between Realism and Romanticism. So far as Romanticism meant facile and copious sentiment, he supported the other side, though his novels lacked Dickens' humor more than the tears. When the debate looked simplest, he formulated it as between "mind and emotion" or between the "realistic type, searching for what to it seems the truth, and the romantic type searching for what will give it emotional satisfaction."[11] If there is any doubt that his pairing used "emotion" pejoratively, it lapses with his saying that his "heart" may have been "romantic" during his Harvard days but his mind had even then fought to "harmonize the subjective impression with the corrective conviction of the world as it is." This statement jibes with his most useful position, which rested on the tonic effect of dispelling illusion and the dangers of tolerating it. His longest analysis of Romantic fiction, for a public lecture written in 1924, charged that it inculcates naïve reverence for the status quo, love for the exotic and sugar-coated, and escapism or "lying . . . in order to make life more endurable."[12] Forty years earlier this analysis would have been pugnaciously apropos.

Yet Herrick seldom got pugnacious about the matter. As he implied in saying his heart's instinct was Romantic, he felt ambivalent, suspecting even that his Realism happened through "accident or culture," through his being "brought up" on the European masters. Often enough to approach having a basic position after all, he argued that neither side of the debate was exclusively right, that no matured novelist cleaves to either the "expansive" or the "analytical and intellectual mood," and that each mood always recurs no matter what manifesto wins the day. To his particular loss, he never stood for long on the conviction that Realism is the best program for fiction. Yet whatever lasting power he owns came from his swings toward the Realist camp. His verdict that too dogged a Realism leads to "inferior and unimaginative" fiction but that the opposite mode "easily becomes nonsense" held true, in any case, for his work.

No matter how stubborn the feeling that the Realist mode "did not satisfy my whole nature, did not satisfactorily explain all life," the label Romantic made him more restive. He preferred a term favored during the 1880's by those who would not defend Romanticism yet hankered for a milder creed than unrelieved Realism. "Idealism" came to serve as the *nom de guerre* for fiction that suggests the pain but also the aspiration, the soiled flesh but also the soul of humankind, the myriad defeats but also the dream of triumph. The term, with its long history and countless uses, was imprecise; unavailingly, Frank Norris tried to replace it with his brand of "Naturalism," which synthesized Howells and Zola. For twenty or thirty years idealism figured in the critical wars to the confusion of some observers, then and later.

In his typical looseness with terms, Herrick mostly added to the confusion. At times he used "idealistic" for literature that captures the "essence of character and experience" rather than their surfaces and that therefore expresses "inner, hidden, universal truth."[13] His freshest example of this mode, which Howells approvingly separated from the "romanticistic," was the work of Eugene O'Neill, which moves "away from the study of the particular or the group, the ephemeral, the temporary, the individual in short with all his tiresome repetitions of peculiarities that are not so tremendously peculiar"; all that, the delight of many fine novelists, was given up to aid revelation of the "type, from the inside" and of the "spirit which animates human beings, ourselves, life in general." This definition had O'Neill's first major plays in view, but it would have included the even more despairing ones ahead. It did not require optimism or hope; but, at other times these became crucial qualities, and most clearly so in a lecture on "The Technique of the Novel" delivered in 1908: "Literary art that presents character and life under the influence of large, uplifting, and ideal motives and impulses, apart from reality, is idealistic. All great art has something of the idealistic mood."

IV *Two Idealistic Flights*

This lecture came just before Herrick's own hortatory peak, set by the two novels after *Together*: *A Life for a Life* and *The Healer*. Earlier, *The Real World*, while eloquent about transcending sex and mere profits, demanded a general revolution in neither ethics nor the economic system. But, by 1907, Herrick was deifying his master-healers, who had a sizable pool of patients. *A Life for a Life* (1910) raised the need and hope of regeneration, both personal and social. However, respect for probability marked even this novel, which has a vein of sordid detail, as well as episodes of the Howellsian commonplace. Leaving no reason for complacency, its kind of uplift differed radically from what the mass audience wanted. It is often as somber and cautionary as Hawthorne's romances, which nicely fit the less uplifting side of Herrick's program for idealism.

He had far poorer success than Hawthorne in creating a way of projecting essences and universals. Though Hawthorne is best in the shorter pieces, which need not sustain very long at a time his stylized world, Herrick was still straining for epic breadth. But two other notions kept him from always supporting his broad canvas with the detail that was a saving grace of *Together*. Concluding that American society had settled into a mold, he decided that particulars were secondary: that sketching the City, for instance, was better than limning a specific metropolis. Concluding also that the vital "background" lay not in the "physical scene" but its "complex human ferment," he decided to present "the results psychologically and spiritually." Both of these decisions could prove sound in practice, but only when the author is aware that any large point in fiction must operate through minute human interplay. *A Life for a Life* unwisely depended on types, proclaimed as such, and on blunt allegory (or at least the capitalizing of key words like "Success").

His inventiveness fell woefully short of carrying off this experiment. In fact, the first two-thirds of *A Life for a Life* merely adapted the plot of *The Real World*. This time, after that catalytic encounter with a silken girl, a poor lad marches directly to the City without benefit of Harvard. Helped by straining coincidences, Hugh Grant climbs upward in the Bank of the Republic, earning his "big chance" at heading a corporation to market electricity—or Power, as Herrick tagged it in the hope of writing symbolically too. But, after Hugh travels to the Capitol, in a chapter titled "Our Canterbury Pilgrims," he discovers a selfish cabal among financiers, the top statesmen, and the courts. Bringing Dante up to date, an "Anarch" next leads Hugh on a tour of the bottom layers: the hovels, the stifling factories, the hellish coal mines. Nauseated by the fruits of Plunder, Hugh renounces—in surely the worst scene Herrick ever published ("The Gulf," Chapter 34)—the silken maiden, who has proved to be the daughter of the kingpin financier. Spurning also the Anarch's message of Hate, he re-embraces the common lot as a clerk in the bank where he had started out. While Herrick then wheels the years along vaguely but swiftly as usual, Hugh struggles with an apocalyptic manuscript and with cancer. Death is hastened by his heroics after an earthquake strikes the City, leaving admonitory ruins and his example to guide a few, including the converted maiden.

Yet, if refocused, *A Life for a Life* could easily have become a valuable novel about the Progressive era. Beneath its heavy-handed, heavy-minded bombast lay some keen insights. For instance, it outreached the two Cowperwood novels in plumbing the defenses of the wealthy and their lawyers and clergymen, whether they preached Social Darwinism (191, 268–69, 283, 310) or a blander creed. The reformers' arguments were searched just as shrewdly. Herrick had obviously kept abreast of the latest commentary, editorial or scholarly.

His best flash of insight leaped beyond the Progressives' fussing over machine politics and the evil "boss." *A Life for a Life* took due notice of grafting United States senators but rated them as cogs in a deeper network. Concurrently, Herrick outlined a political novel, about a president very much like Theodore Roosevelt, but he quit after deciding that the real sources and circuits of power are economic, as the Anarch explained to Hugh in quasi-Marxist terms (80–83). Hugh, who gravitated toward banking, later found that big-time publishing and industrial engineering, for example, were merely its satellites. His valedictory on Life contended that private ownership beats down all other rights, that control of stock and bonds triumphs over physical property, and that the true capitol of the country stands on the richest pile of negotiable capital. He gave no comfort to hopes that the direct primary or popular election of senators would revamp the power structure.

Though Herrick tried some arguments, and even language of Marxist flavor, his critique was basically native in origin. As with Henry Adams, his Puritan heritage left him cool to both the robber baron and the trade unionist; one of his earliest short stories, "Miss Atherton's Mission," let spokesmen for employers and labor hold a fair debate. But he could not go on believing that the struggle itself was fair. He came to suspect that the well-to-do of Chicago had used the courts to lynch the Haymarket anarchists. (The future Mrs. Herrick was among the fashionable ladies invited by the presiding judge to look on from the bench.) During the campaign of 1896, after Herrick had listened coldly to William Jennings Bryan, a University of Chicago economist convinced him that the hard-money Republicans were cynically unsound. As for foreign policy, Lovett, quoting friends in the State Department, reported in 1898 that Spain had wanted to avoid the war; it was demanded by our "rotten" Congress because of chauvinism and general greed.[14] However, *The Web of Life* and even *The Memoirs of an American Citizen* had treated the Spanish-American War uncritically. Herrick's radicalism, evolving thoughtfully from his firm ethic, was not yet urgent.

Featuring the Pullman strike of 1894, *The Web of Life* actually leaned toward the right in stressing vandalism and venal union leaders; and the anarchist intent on murder in the *Memoirs* was suited for readers in ormolu parlors. Yet the suffering on the bottom rung was pressing Herrick away from the hair-raising myths of the reactionaries. Around 1907 he had an impulse to write a "new Ring & the Book over the Moyer-Haywood case . . . where story is told of labor conspiracy from point of view of Capital, Labor, Wife of miner, Grafting Politician, Upright Judge." Revealingly, he still could not decide whose viewpoint "must Rule in the chaos of the world."

But the muckrakers, who had started the Anarch on his path in *A Life for a Life*, finally tipped the scale. Two short stories of 1911–12 proved that Herrick, combative earlier, had moved with the resurgent wave of their exposures. The first, "Found Out," declared that the giants of business and finance break the law regularly, with fear only of publicity. The second, "His Leetle Trees," concerned an insolent and corrupt gas company that left its humble victims little recourse but violence; this story (for *Everybody's Magazine*) gave his most credible portrait so far of the plebeians. Short on credibility, *A Life for a Life* tried to make full amends on the count of sympathy.

As with so many intellectuals after the era of Grantism, Herrick's vision of the American dream had initially lacked warmth for the common man. In the 1890's, he questioned the worth of "making the beds a little better" or helping the "unfortunate to slide through" life. It took the redeemed Isabelle Lane of *Together* to warn that in the "millions" stifled by poverty lurked an "infinite variety" of "possibilities" that justify the "hope and the faith for a Democracy" (528). Yet the idea of democracy is seldom held purely in total defiance of the milieu. Herrick's new concern for the masses sprang partly from current fretting about national "vitality," which would decline if they were kept mired in privation. From a wider angle, marked by the red-eyed Anarch, he feared that the masses, if spurned too long, would erupt into another Reign of Terror, demanding a "life for a life." But the heaviest drag on his democracy was doubt—to be renounced in his final book—that the average man, however deserving of sympathy, is very educable (168, 241).

The selflessness common in the ruins of the earthquake proved mostly temporary. Beneath its humane fervor *A Life for a Life* gave no grounds for faith in mass action, thus leaving—as John Chamberlain observes in *Farewell to Reform*—"the central problem—the problem of the approach to power—untouched."

Nor did Herrick pose any economic or political revolution that the elite should engineer. No matter how lopsided the tug-of-war between the rich and poor looked, he circled back to self-reform as the chief solution (348, 427–28), whether disguised as altruistic immolation or as ascetic contempt of Success. As he told his publisher, the key concept of *A Life for a Life* was "individualism." He saw no other clear avenue while assuming, like most of his contemporaries, the need to end with a solution. He could not rest with the American paradox of trusting both private conscience and the latent wisdom of the majority, nor could he build on the tension between them. But his growing respect for the ordinary man brought fuller warmth and enriched his future work.

Unfortunately, the technique of *A Life for a Life* promised little for the future. A critic hungry for comfort can praise only patches, such as a portrait widely taken to satirize Nicholas Murray Butler, president of

Columbia University, or the treatment of the Bank of the Republic as a live entity in the manner of Frank Norris. Before the fever of creation ebbed, Herrick insisted that *A Life for a Life* held "much of the best writing I have ever done, or ever can hope to do." If nothing else, the landscape passages were first-rate, he felt sure; but our generation finds them verbose as well as too evidently symbolic, in keeping with his battering approach, while his irony was so coarse as to become melodrama.

Around 1913, in the vein of Thorstein Veblen, Herrick made sardonic notes on the idea that every society develops its "Mandarins," or privileged class, with a "profusion of possession, a dilettante interest in art and literature and music, a fondness for sports, a love of change . . . a feeling of possession—*mine*." *A Life for a Life* would have profited from the cool tone of these notes. Too easily, Herrick's weak sense of comedy was being held in check, as his next novel betrayed almost as disastrously.

The operatic and exalted moods in *The Healer* (1911) are especially irritating because they purport to fit a tough-minded goal. The peak of ecstasy (the "highest stimulus of romantic circumstance") at which Eric Holden, a physician who chose exile in the backwoods, marries a beautiful heiress, whom he saved with a masterly operation, soon erodes toward mundane discord. For, though Herrick (who echoed his name in Eric) was searching for his own soul mate and sketching prose poems on his ideal of romantic love, *The Healer* asserted that a fall from its heights is inevitable. With passion clouding his saturnine judgment, Holden expects the heiress to share his austerity in a rough-hewn camp. As the "golden dust of illusion" rubs away, she thickens into a matron who wants a luxurious home, the company of her old set, the latest advantages for her brood, and status for her husband; she forces him to exploit his talent by building a large hospital, which helps bring the railroad and other juggernauts of progress. Prodded by a devastating fire, Eric saves what is left of his gifts by deserting his family and doing penance among the urban poor. His wife, pensively but unwaveringly, reverts to all the habits of her clan. (When Monogram Pictures made its scenario of the novel in 1935, a reconciliation was surely added.)

A corollary guide for the plot was that women, by nature, chill any noble aspirations: "Tradition has taught them for generations to work by fraud and wile, and their instinct warns them against the ideal. All prolonged contest with them will end in the deterioration of the man" (274). When Hugh Grant chose revolt as his mistress, *A Life for a Life* agreed that the "end of no man's being is a woman, however adored and desired." Ignoring the hope of partnership that *Together* extended, *The Healer* made the female's pursuit of cozy security almost too powerful for a superman. This indictment, building toward a climax in Hemingway's war on the emasculating woman, had ancient roots; some males surely pitied themselves in the most patriarchial societies ever seen. Still, the onrushing emancipation of women gave it urgency and sweep. In Wells's *Marriage*, a spending wife pulls a husband stronger than Holden away from pure research. A new cliché of plot had been born.

Despite Herrick's disdain for "problem" novels, *The Healer* agitated another current issue (which has returned to trouble our day). *The Web of Life* had protested against leaving medical care to the pressures and abuses of profit. *Together* more directly asked the state to cure the taint of commercialism by underwriting treatment for everybody. Strained by heavy bills for the last few years, Herrick was vehement in *The Healer*, having Holden confess: "A doctor who makes fifty thousand dollars a year as I have done has coined his soul and sold it" (384). After redemption, Holden called in detail for unstinting care supported "by society as a whole for its own preservation and betterment" (418). Happily for the medical profession, Herrick, partly by design but also because of unruly qualms, made Holden one of his least attractive idealists.

The profession, just getting its house in solid order, could also shrug off Holden because he was marginal, if not clinically disreputable. Often he works as a faith-healer dispensing the "joy of perfect will"; while Herrick adds confusion by deriding the Freudian search for "hidden sorrows," Holden dabbles even in psychiatry, which was merely beginning to win respect in the United States (266, 282, 421, 435). At other times, he prescribes altruism as the high road to wholeness, with help from the "old Puritan themes of sin, self-sacrifice, and regeneration."[15] Whether from a rebounding Realism, however, or a falling measure of what the individualist can achieve, Herrick ended with his hero much subdued. Enlarging the most effective motif in *The Web of Life*, the second half of *The Healer* stressed the grinding weight of "change, always change in the restless dance of will and desire" as the possibility of "rare beauty . . . somehow faded inevitably along the way" (237). Herrick never again trumpeted that a realm of perfect will and action is attainable: he had accepted the view and the universe of twentieth-century man.

This decline of faith in practicable absolutes soon led to vibrant irony on floundering in the imperfect flux and to a welcome lowering of pitch. Herrick no longer used punitive flames so grossly as in *The Healer*, where the moral is expounded while Holden's debased sanitarium burns down. Nor would he put such bald faith in the spirituality of the great open spaces, which Jack London had made so fashionable that even the scientist and his wife in Wells's *Marriage* trek the frozen North to rediscover their essential selves. More largely, Herrick's attempt to fashion an Ibsen-like Realism, in which elemental characters and settings soar into universal symbols, was over. Before long, with shallow yet healthy insight, he dismissed his two most hortatory novels as "Hawthornesque and also didactic, ghostly and therefore inartistic."

V   *A Pot Boiler*

Before regaining his firmest stride, Herrick wasted time with a "rickety romance," *His Great Adventure* (1913). Though serialized in a popular magazine, it sold just passably as a book and for sound reasons. It has a few worthwhile passages, notably those drawing on the unforgettable weeks he once spent in Mexico and the wan coterie of sharpsters he observed there. However, the readers who could enjoy the pellmell plot cared little for honest vignettes or for a chapter of informed satire on sponsors of "good causes." On the other hand, even the escapist reader may have found the web of coincidence too wide and thick in the action which involves a struggling author. He helps a dying stranger, is plunged into racing across the continent, then flees through the Southwest and to Europe with a wad of securities; once he cashes them and earns more millions, he searches for the rightful heiress, who actually is already at hand because—but additional summary wastes time and effort.

Any shrewd reader finds at least two deeper flaws. In expanding a manuscript left over from 1906, Herrick at times sounded enchanted again with the man of business and therefore of "action, power"; for contrast, he denigrated the intellectual and even the writer who deals with shadowy words rather than dividend-yielding objects (205, 209). Yet the hero, when grown affluent, subsidizes the People's Theater, a plan to found repertory groups to perform quality plays at low box-office prices. (In the *Saturday Evening Post* of March 31, 1906, Herrick had supported an endowed "national theater.") In a second inconsistency, *His Great Adventure* sets out to argue that the masses, if given the chance, will pay for first-rate drama; but it ultimately decides that they already get the level of fare they deserve: the People's Theater collapses like the richly endowed New Theater venture of 1901 that it resembles. This wavering is perhaps forgivable; for ten years Herrick had been yearning to emerge as a pace-setting dramatist, but had discovered that hardly anybody, producer or audience, thought he should. His unpublished plays are, in fact, too poor to discuss.

Herrick's public served him well by its reluctance to buy not only his "rickety romance" but also *A Life for a Life* and *The Healer*. It thus helped to discourage him in 1913 from carrying out , for example, a novel planned to have four "movements" like a symphony, executed in an "idealistic and poetic manner." With sounder taste than Herrick attributed to his readers in *His Great Adventure*, his public preferred the vein he worked best. In a self-analysis during 1915 Herrick concluded that while "once in so often" he "was due to go on a bust and think" himself "an heir of all the poets and life a matter of mystery and music," he was essentially a Realist. By then, he would have proved to be one better than ever before.

CHAPTER 4

Resolutions

Never again did Herrick waver so badly in taste or purpose as he had in *His Great Adventure*. Though his working notes and some of his public opinions still made confusing patterns, he regained his sureness as a novelist just when Western culture was staggering toward a world war that upset the certainties of many intellectuals. Most notably his fiction resolved its indecisions concerning method. Furthermore, it moved to fresh perspectives on human nature and society.

The clearest statement of his return to more productive trails came in "The American Novel" (in the *Yale Review* for April, 1914), which conceded that the New England mind, with Howells as its last heir, had lost authority. This admission marked a permanent decline in his stress on the power of ethical absolutes and also a restrictive shift in the content of his own absolutes. In positive terms, these changes encouraged a keener receptivity to the "richest background in a purely human way that the story-teller ever had offered him," a background teeming with "new notes of character, of situation, of theme, of human drama . . . religious and pagan, selfish and generous, adventurous and mean, sordid and splendid,— at one and the same time." While Herrick's claim was narrowly American in its view of the uniqueness of our culture, it was liberating, for his next two novels achieved a fresh level of secular, good-natured vigor.

This vigor was held back from its own excesses by a firmer standard of accountability. For in a column in the Chicago *Tribune* of March 22, 1914, he warned: "In the long run, we must live by truth—, truth to fact, truth to feeling, and truth to life as it is." Like the full-blown Realists, Herrick had matured also into the corollary belief that the truth had not yet been told fully, that a master of "girth and insight" was still needed to "put the spade down into the sub-soil . . . delving beneath the convention-al, the expected, the Victorian." Instead of demanding that such delving uncover a realm of ideality, he invoked the principle—spacious enough for old and new masterworks of fiction—that the "primary function of the imagination always is, not to entertain, not to preach a moral, but to realize our world for us, to make us see and feel what we are too dull or too preoccupied to realize for ourselves."[1] This drive to re-create or unveil life in the round rather than lead the way toward essences gave *One*

Woman's Life (1913) its engaging yet substantial effect, one not too far short of greatness.

I *A Happy Madame Bovary*

In "The American Novel" Herrick wondered why his countrymen had produced so little fiction that could be honestly acclaimed as great. Among other reasons, he blamed tendencies to center on the prosperous or even the leisurely rather than the hard-working majority, to blur the facts of sex, and to sentimentalize all facts from those of "success and business warfare" to the "amorous relation of the sexes and the home." *One Woman's Life* tried to counteract each of these tendencies, but it cannot be labeled a "business" novel though its readers ponder little about other patterns of success so long as Milly Ridge holds the stage. Like the main line of Herrick's males, her husband wastes his talent—for painting, this time—in order to get dollars; but he is primarily a facet of Milly's self-seeking, which bends everything to its ends.

Between 1911 and 1913, Herrick, his health and energy renewed, had worked at a multivolumed treatment of the "family"; for he believed himself the "one" novelist "competent" to "deal with that Sacred Cow." Revolted by his mother's ambitions, he had long suspected that many, if not most, women used the family as a tool to establish their status—and expended parents and husbands and children in the process. Self-tuned to social gradations from the outset, Milly gaily but relentlessly schemes toward keeping up with the "best" circles. She climbs far higher than her widowed father's manners and modest paycheck make likely by calculating every move such as switching her church membership whenever she sees a chance to improve her connections. Endowed with tea-party "charm," she campaigns to the verge of a brilliant catch before rushing into a romantic marriage with an artist. Once youthful ardor cools, however, she pushes her husband into exhaustion and fatal pneumonia by her hunger for the prodigal marks of success. While not cynical, much less icily conniving, Milly's social career always saps her loyalty to the family hearth.

In 1913, Herrick also drafted his vaguely humorous play, *The Second Fall of Man*; in it a matriarchy grows so self-centered that it decides even to arrange for reproduction without male help. Less drastically, in *One Woman's Life* a victim saw Milly as an "adventuress . . . a fortuitous, somewhat parasitic creature . . . 'a little grafter'" (404). Still unable to forgo lengthy comment, Herrick particularly flayed her "pleasant illusion . . . that she was altogether a superior creation—something mysterious to be worshipped and preserved" (32—33). This illusion guided her narcissistic indulgences and lulled her male victims into tolerating them. In the Realistic tradition of correcting popular taste, much of the blame for Milly's mind was laid at the door of nineteenth-century literature: Milly found her fatuous image confirmed in "Tennyson and in every novel as well as in the few plays she saw." Though Herrick's notes for a love-epic with a strain of Victorian fervor had mounted, he plunged on to a Darwinist taunt that she never suspected that "her long, thick hair with its glint of gold, her soft eyes, her creamy skin and rounding breasts and sloping thighs were all designed for the simple purpose of continuing the species."

This jeer recognized that Milly's illusion could not be fought without questioning her ethereal purity or, more generally, the current "prudery in the sex realm." Herrick's "The American Novel" ventured that "probably more than half of the larger issues of living are affected in one way or another by the sex impulse—at least are colored by it"; without hiding behind either Howells or Freud, he argued that the impressionable maiden "will get less harm from *Madame Bovary* than from perusing one of our sentimental boy-and-girl stories." His notes for *One Woman's Life* prescribed "an American Madame Bovary against Sentimentalism," though "without sex irregularity." The concession to moralism was not fatal or deep; in fact, Milly's husband has a comforting affair with a Russian baroness. While Milly never takes sexual chances, she has—said the working notes—"really lively passions." In *The Healer* Holden caressed his wife with a hungriness that was "troubling, disturbing, and yet intoxicating to her" (235); but Milly responds to her husband more cheerfully and kinetically.

Her one questionable link is with Ernestine Geyer, who ably runs a commercial laundry. Charmed with her beribboned fluffiness, Ernestine ends the financial rout of Milly's widowhood by supporting her as the mistress of their joint housekeeping. Before long, Milly lures the spinster into backing her scheme of catering expensive French pastry—a superbly typical venture for her. Having guided their bakery into collapse, she blithely flits to golden California with an orange-grower who was spurned ten years earlier. Despite some references to the liaison with mannish Ernestine as a "marriage," it fills out the range of Milly's selfishness rather than her sexuality. One of Herrick's long-time favorites was Maupassant's *Bel-Ami*, in which an opportunist capitalizes on his sexual magnetism. Just as easy with her conscience, Milly is much less roughshod and never uses allure by design, but her triumphs are recounted with Maupassant's sardonic pleasure in crassness that defies pious maxims.

For the first time since some early stories, Herrick sounded more amused than outraged: he was smiling more over man's stupidity than growling at his corruption. Yet, taken in another way, *One Woman's Life* opened up a colder approach: while its characters are not loudly or aggressively evil, few deserve much respect, and nobody learns much from his mistakes or finds conversion from his narrow self-seeking. In other words, Herrick did not belabor human nature shrilly because he now expected less from it. However contrary to the moral optimism of the Progressive era, this wry mellowing, curious for its suddenness, was attractive in his case.

Easily more admirable than Milly at least, Ernestine marked a simpler turn in his feelings. Like the Yankee Brahmins, he had thus far slighted the sweating worker and especially the immigrant, had been almost as guilty as Milly in ignoring that "Chicago was a huge pool into which all races and peoples drained" and that the "hordes of these savage-looking foreigners" toiled brutally in the factories and slaughterhouses (71). Growingly aware of his blindness, he had been inching his way with mostly wooden results. His first wage earner to emerge completely (others had served as background), Ernestine is staunchly vivid in her unpolished yet honest manners, her courage toward a deformity caused by a shop accident, and her strong-voiced reliance on making ends meet by doing the world's dirty labor (laundry, preferably). Herrick never matched Dreiser as an observer of the grimy tenements, but his novels from 1913 on gave some reasonably fair glimpses. Hereafter he could with better grace again reprove Edith Wharton for concentrating on the "smart set" and warn young novelists that the lowly and foreign-born can also have social relations.

Ernestine has further force because she carried Herrick's attitude on the increasingly live question of female rights. Dimly favoring such privileges in principle after years at the University of Chicago, which championed higher education for women, he was skeptical in practice. *One Woman's Life* sneered at the rhetoric of suffragism and at the jeweled matrons spouting it. On a potentially incisive point, he made a diversionary tactic of contending, like Edward Bellamy, that economic equality, to be earned by performance, is the key to political rights. This twist at least led him to play up Ernestine's stalwart competence and to discourage laced-handkerchief weeping over her hard knocks. Though few suffragettes were likely to join her in competing at rough-fisted jobs, she quickened the vitality of action with her every appearance. And, because Herrick had the restraint to drop her in mid-career, the full circle of her fate was left to challenging speculation.

He succeeded almost as well with Milly's other victims. Both as a small-time salesman and a subdued failure, her father exudes a Realistic aura; Grandma Ridge, dun yet feline, holds credible surprises; Jack Bragdon escapes from bathos to soft-keyed tragedy as a talented painter drowning in the magazine world; in surprising contrast, Clive Reinhard, a popular novelist and therefore a likely target for caricature, has a cryptic integrity and refreshing aplomb. But, since Herrick had returned to the convention of building around a main figure, *One Woman's Life* must stand or fall with Milly. She is always convincing, from her debut in a crudely varnished parlor to her exit on the Sunshine Special that she boards with a second husband, whose proposal she had accepted placidly over a fine dinner. Having sinned more deeply but respectably than Dreiser's Carrie Meeber, she is more plausibly free of remorse, as free— Herrick told a pained guardian of morals—as Helen of Troy who reaped a "very proper and comfortable end to it all."

Most readers can enjoy Milly even while yearning for her comeuppance. Before her egotism proves tameless, her petty ambitions arouse the sympathy that youth can usually count upon. Later, she comes disarmingly close to learning from a few of her mistakes and achieves a fleeting humility when she decides to be happy that her exploited first husband found solace with an understanding mistress. Between the peaks of her success, moralists can savor reverses that genially but momentarily deflate Milly, as when she learns that she is too short between knee and hip to be a studio model. Furthermore, her private habits and quirks are set down indelibly. Part of the unflagging humor of *One Woman's Life* rides between the reader's knowledge of Milly and the glamorized picture held by her admirers.

Herrick's ease, never equalled again, in animating a heroine's commonplaces had an obvious source; he drew heavily on his wife—the last straw on her bundle of grievances, and they separated for good. Yet the surehandedness of *One Woman's Life* is not so simple to attain, or it would be swamped by competitors. As Herrick pointed out to the documentary school of Realists, only artful selection of detail can raise fiction above a turgid transcript.[2] Short on inventiveness and slow to project beneath the skin of others, he had winnowed and adapted from his wife's idiosyncrasies so deftly that only her friends could suspect rancor or mere copying. Though he conceived of *One Woman's Life* as a return to "social history," Milly and her ambiance were drawn with economic strokes. Though distinctive, she managed to suggest that her milieu would continue to shape other Milly Ridges.

As if purged by his idealistic "binge," Herrick did almost everything right for the moment. Better than ever before, he paced *One Woman's Life* through a lengthwise plot without the effect of cramming or breakneck rushing. Likewise, the novel struck a cleanly ironic tone in the first pages, never came near to losing poise, and ended with an air of reflective amusement that would have done credit to Thackeray, whom it probably had in mind more than Flaubert. In 1910, Herrick jotted: "Light and comic material—the only note to use with the realistic world." For a timeless precept this would be of course too restrictive and too likely to breed flippancy, but at that stage of his development the guideline was refreshingly sound. It helped his next step reach almost as close to major achievement.

II *A Comedy of Social Criticism*

Considering Herrick's proneness to switch directions within a novel, the comic note held gratifyingly far into the pages of *Clark's Field* (1914). Made distinct from the author at the outset, its narrator is sophisticated, cosmopolitan, and ripely wise despite traces of Herrick's old hauteur in adjectives like "vulgar" or "unrefined." Its sardonic touches challenge silly illusions rather than bad manners, as when it observes that an American who is puttering in Paris ateliers assumed he was bound to succeed because he was enduring poverty. Likewise, the issues are not narrowly or oppressively moral, especially at first. As "The American Novel" implored his contemporaries to do, Herrick had broadened his horizons; and the pleasure of mere discovery was prominent.

The opening chapters—with the rickety devotees of the Grand Army of the Republic, the plush temple of the trust company and its silky deacons, the palatial finishing school for shallow girls—establish a teeming background for the ordeal of Adelle Clark, the unwitting center of manifold ironies. A colorless girl of fourteen who cleans up after threadbare roomers, she is enriched by a freak of inheritance in what becomes a sly updating of the Cinderella story. Jewels and furs transform her into an exotic bloom that quickly draws admirers; once her starved mind and heart settle on a feckless and untalented painter, she insists on an elopement since she is becoming used to having her wishes gratified. But the ironic reversals have just begun: she coddles her Prince Charming so lavishly that he soon asserts his dignities and then vices as a man of wealth; this change eventually arouses her to plumb their situation and divorce him, leaving him more soured and helpless than when love brought a golden tide. Only Herrick's first book, *The Man Who Wins*, had such capacity for wryness.

The wryness in *Clark's Field* was more stinging, however, because it touched a vital nerve, that of private property. Herrick had been studying

Henry George or his disciples on the unearned increment of land values, had been listening to enemies of wealth by inheritance, and had been shuddering over the amusements and political clichés of the rich. The narrator says of Tom Clark, a capable stonemason who tasted few luxuries even in California: "He was far too intelligent to believe what the Sunday School taught, and the average American thinks he believes, that property and position in this world are apportioned by desert of one sort or another" (441). This belief is concretely tested by the rise of Clark's cousin Adelle. By-product of a foolish marriage, she emerges as sole heir to fifty acres that a legal tangle kept from being sold long before her birth and before the spillover of a metropolis boomed their value dizzyingly. Even so, she gets her windfall only because a quixotic judge wonders why a team of sleek lawyers hovers around a shabby child. No virtue of her own, obviously, earns any of the wealth that inflates her prestige and self-esteem.

Herrick made Adelle's fortune grow by the millions without her help or concern. But, aware that the great entrepreneurs had bred heirs intent on glittering consumption rather than on epical if greedy schemes, he fixed the spotlight on her new peers, measuring their fiber not by the Brahmin ethic but the standards of her rearing among Yankee plebeians. In sober retrospect, her years as apprentice housemaid had more basis for dignity than those in which she fritters away her dividends. The very ease with which she attains the role of princess when she can foot the bill offers another mordant probe of status. The irony compounds when she finally decides that her peers in extravagance did her poor service on every score.

This vein is saved from vapidity by awareness that the grind of privation is much harsher, nevertheless, than the burdens of overfed play. Tacitly recanting much of his fiction, Herrick dismissed the "heroic creed" that the "struggle of poverty was the way of salvation" (364). Both at the opening before Adelle's pumpkin turns to gold and near the end when Tom Clark, perched on a box in his tarpaper shanty, details the back-breaking routine at his depths, just how painfully the masses toil is made graphic. When Adelle abandons luxury, she pulls up well short of re-embracing the common lot. Herrick's grasp of its miseries now avoided the delusions of the privileged. He grew almost lyrical in pity for the immigrants swarming in the tenements hastily raised on Clark's "field" when it could be "developed." But he also did Tom Clark the justice of respecting his hostile cynicism and drinking sprees.

In many ways, *Clark's Field* was more studiedly antisentimental than *One Woman's Life*. It belabored a fashionable school for girls—Herndon Hall—as the nastiest culmination of the rationale that shaped Milly Ridge;

it brushed over the courtship of Adelle and her fiancé, explaining that they merely repeated the banalities of young lovers. Warning that "single motives are more rarely found in life than in art" (120), it traced a tangle of purposes in any character with a plausible claim to depth. For the first time, Freudian terms crept into Herrick's judgments, though they were used superficially and cautiously. A sane reviewer for the *Dial* (of July 1, 1914) concluded that Herrick was flouting the popular "demand for heroes and heroines" and that he "never completely forgets that his obligations to his public include that of educating it."

Unfortunately, this compliment was not wholly deserved. Somewhere past the middle of *Clark's Field*, Herrick began relaxing his narrator's ironic drive and his skepticism toward paragons of virtue. When last seen, Tom Clark still lags well short of perfection; but the judge who gives Adelle valedictory advice struck Howells as "almost too consolingly righteous for entire belief." While Howells had no complaints about the reformed heroine, she irritated Randolph Bourne, who protested that "it is becoming more and more embarrassing to read an American novel"; he could not help "blushing" at the patness with which her lost cousin appears or guessing "immediately that she would have to be redeemed and share her wealth."[3] No one except Dreiser, rasped Bourne—who evidently had not read *One Woman's Life*—could resist the solution of spiritual rebirth. Just opening his crusade for cosmopolitan morality and intellectual toughness, Bourne was anticipating the reaction that discarded most American fiction published before the 1920's.

More immediately, Bourne was so sulky, perhaps, because Adelle had started out so viably, both as a satiric foil and as a wispy atom of humanity, and because her creator failed to justify her recoil from lolling on velvet. After a weak try, Herrick lamely fell back on her intimations from an "unknown," divine force. He had far more glaring trouble in laying out a course for the redeemed Adelle, who is wary of loosing a windfall on others but feels called to share her wealth with society and especially the once lost branch of the Clarks. When last seen, she plans to build a bathhouse for the tenements on the developed land and to investigate her relatives before spending money on them—even to use it, if advisable, to expose their crimes. If the Jehovah-like twist is ignored—it cannot be dismissed as planted naiveté—*Clark's Field* still stands guilty of having "resolutely avoided the radical implications" of its social criticism and of ending with the "most traditional of solutions—private charity to the worthy poor—" when its socioeconomic analysis seems "to demand a conclusion in terms of political and economic reform, or even revolution."[4]

Herrick hoped Adelle would seem less of an egret-feathered angel if hardheaded Tom Clark became her deputy, but their teamwork raises the promise of a standard lovers' match. Arthur Guiterman rebelled in one of his "Rhymed Reviews" for the comic-weekly *Life*:

> Belike she'll marry Thomas when
> They've settled Minor Circumstances,
> If this is Realism, then
> I wish you'd tell me what Romance is.[5]

An answer to this jeer might invoke Herrick's creed of "idealism" again. Or, more simply, he might, like Howells, invoke his recurring faith in "essential health and sanity" as the note that reached Americans better than the "bestiality and insanity" of a Zola.[6] However, as with the last part of *Adventures of Huckleberry Finn*, no flourish of theory will save impartial, serious readers from feeling let down. Since escapist readers were jangled by the main plot, sales were disappointing.

All in all, nevertheless, *Clark's Field* was a noble effort. Herrick's intellectual and social grasp was still expanding along with, more slowly, his esthetics. In the spring of 1914 before the novel appeared, "How to Write"—the best in a loose series of columns for the Chicago *Tribune*—concluded that "there are as many 'techniques' as there are kinds of materials or ideas to be handled. . . . Technique is always a question of bringing out all the possibilities in a subject in a way most possible for a writer." Recent theorists about fiction agree, and yet *Clark's Field* went no further than a confident mastery of pre-Joycean conventions. Its pattern clearly belongs to a staider age even without the scene in which Tom risks his neck for Adelle's child during a fire. But Herrick's society was about to quake at its foundations, and he never again wrote such an old-fashioned rescue scene after his resolve to quit supporting the war that had started in the late summer of 1914.

III   *World War I*

In a stock-taking lecture on "The Drift of Political Opinion," composed in the winter of 1922–23, Herrick said that the outbreak of war "absorbed" him in current events for the first time. The undramatic truth is that absorption had set in earlier, even before he began making long visits to Washington in 1913. One of his *Tribune* columns proclaimed him a Democrat—strong omen of change for a son of "cold roast beef Boston," as his youngest sister tagged their background. Another column opened with, "I commonly think of myself as being somewhat of a Socialist";

though derisive toward the "preposterous assumptions" of the militants, Herrick welcomed the "delightfully impudent" *Masses*, which was less Marxist than iconoclastic. Such comments indicate he was ready to learn from minority views on the war after the first waves of righteousness had subsided.

Herrick's viewpoint was nevertheless orthodox enough for the *Tribune* editors to hire him as a foreign correspondent in 1915. Also, they evidently felt he had shown the necessary breadth. He had responded finally to the Progressives' interacting sense of imminent showdowns and openings for basic advance, as well as to their warning that huge problems called for expertly informed solutions. He now perceived a fresh weld of monopoly economics and organized labor and social science, which broke qualitatively with familiar patterns. In 1915, groping for perspective, he took the first major inventory of his past with "Myself," which regretted that Harvard had taught him nothing "about so many subjects that have interested me since,–biology, economics, especially." Unknowingly, he was preparing to desert the genteel intellectuals who preached that the war posed the apocalyptic test between cultured or moral absolutes and Teutonic savagery.

But Herrick's desertion was delayed and confused by his lingering faith in the American dream. His first public reaction invoked pride in our unique prosperity, reached without the street fighting and the wars of decadent Europe. This doctrine of American transcendence over "narrow, arrogant nationalism" held until he went abroad in the spring of 1915. Later he accused his faculty colleagues of having rushed to Washington in 1917 because they were bored with the musty groves of academe, but he anticipated their desire to prove capable of virile endeavors as all fine values seemed to tremble before the boots of Junker militarism and only the rarest skeptics kept their balance.

By the October 30 issue of the *New Republic* Herrick's "Recantation of a Pacifist" rang with exhortings such as, "War is a great developer as well as a destroyer of life." In a quieter key "The Conscript Mother" (for *Scribner's Magazine* of May, 1916) praised the eager Allied recruits (and their stiff-lipped parents) in an Italy missing from Hemingway's *A Farewell to Arms.* This story-sketch was shrewdly rushed into a hard-cover reprint.

Herrick's loudest blow for the Allies was *The World Decision* (1916), based on his *Tribune* dispatches from Italy and France. It reveals that old personal wars had fed his militancy. Its hatred of German "materialism" obliquely carried on his hostility to the worship of success and practical results; in promoting defeat for Germany, the United States could, he hoped, exorcise its worst self. Still *The World Decision* is not worth threshing, though it tried to be judicious and was capably, sometimes brilliantly written. Our rhetoric from World War I seems emptier than that from any other period of cannonading, and Herrick's "Introduction" to *Poèmes des Poilus* (1917), published for the New England Branch of the American Fund for French Wounded, also holds nothing but blatant overuse of "chivalry" as the key term.

His fervor had inevitably lashed out at soft-headed neutralists. To their rage, Herrick started his change from militancy as opinion at home swung toward intervention. Allowed to become an insider because of his militant pen, he had already "seen too much, heard too much, knew too much." On February 7, while Congress took the last steps toward combat, he recorded privately: "More and more convinced that the U.S. should not mix in European politics"; and he backed his conclusion with an analysis of the war as a result of "commercial ambitions" that were intensified by the "rapid growth of industrialism."[7] Furthermore, he still cherished his vision of the United States as superior to Old World butchery. Like Woodrow Wilson, he had hoped to tip the balance with moral and mental logistics. Our formal entry into war set him to glooming that the world had gone "mad" and, less melodramatically, that the nation he had trusted in for almost fifty years was showing "abysmal faults."

As the United States pointed its energy toward Europe, Herrick took the backtrail to the University of Chicago, where he grimly enjoyed a recommitment to the timeless goals of the humanities. Yet he could not let the world run without his advice; and, though seeming to herald the disillusion that struck the 1920's, he stayed above nihilism, personal or social. He worked actively on "Tomorrow," an attempt to forecast the postwar world and to guide it away from another imperialistic cycle. As an immediate countermove, he defended Henri Barbusse's *Le Feu* from the censors who feared its Realism about the suffering in the trenches. "Unromantic War," an essay for the *Dial* of February 14, 1918, pleaded for facing up to the horror and waste so that humanity would shrink away from future carnage. Herrick's many personal enemies must have raged that he was never in step.

They could say the same about his part in the postwar election. "For Hoover," an editorial in the *Nation* (June 5, 1920), intoned: "I am an internationalist (and therefore a pacifist), a philosophical radical (or parlor Bolshevist, if you prefer the sneer), and something more than a skeptic as to the divine origin of the capitalistic system." While vaguely convinced that our economy was doomed, he suggested that Herbert Hoover would in the meantime give it the most efficient steering. After the Republican nomination went to Warren Harding, he damned both major parties;

"Normalcy" left him hostile in spite of word that the President admired *The Web of Life* and *The Healer*. Intent on the lessons of the late holocaust, Herrick helped spread the argument that it had been "merely an extension and intensification of peace-time principles" which must be reshaped.

Though he had vowed on February 8, 1917—the day after his separate peace—to return to the "noble field of art—humanity's best relief," he took a long time getting back to fiction. Friendlier than ever with Lovett, who was now an editor of the *New Republic*, Herrick wrote political essays, tried to visit the Soviet Union (as the dancer Isadora Duncan's "secretary," if need be), and considered a biography of Homer Lea, the racist soldier of fortune. In the winter of 1922—23, a set of three informed lectures on the "drift" of political, economic, and social thought gave weight to his assertion that he was "vastly more interested" in world affairs than in belles lettres, that his reading had turned to "business, economics, philosophy and the social sciences." Tying literature closely to society, three succeeding lectures accused the Romantic spirit of feeding nationalistic drives while the Realist labored to explode current delusions. One crucial delusion Herrick kept questioning was that of unilateral German villainy; in a kind of valedictory on the war, he summarized exposures of how the Allies had duped their masses with propaganda. Still, with tenacious faith in erring mankind, he looked forward to educating "human nature as it can be"—increasingly his rallying cry.[8]

IV *A Healthy Madame Bovary*

The return to literature with *Homely Lilla* (1923) was, surprisingly, neither an escape to the "relief" of art nor a highly topical commentary. Herrick's attemps to heighten debate on burning issues had forced him to conclude that the "two matters which are most negligible in the psychology of the true American are his religion and his politics." Accordingly, his characters in this novel put their energy mostly into narrow matters with little concern for the stream of public events, which swirled past World War I. Yet these events jostled the characters in small and large ways, and he achieved his soundest play between individuals and the changing milieu. He had too seldom remembered that life itself is the rightful hero of the novel, whose protagonists therefore should not be self-sufficient prodigies; or else, overreacting, he had given historical forces too central or crucial a role. "Strangely unappreciated"—observes Edward Wagenknecht in *Cavalcade of the American Novel* (1952)—*Homely Lilla* avoids both poles of error. More than loyalty to a friend impelled Lovett's opinion (*Dial*,

May, 1923) that Herrick had "gained rather than lost in mastery of his vehicle" during the hiatus of nine years. If nothing else, as Lovett pointed out, Herrick had controlled his usual distortions of emphasis and attained an "easy uniformity of texture."

Unfortunately for its fame, all the achievements of *Homely Lilla* appeared deceptively easy. Herrick's dicta in his *Tribune* column had included: "The one sure thing that really important literature always conveys to me is the unconsciousness of the craftsmanship. Its creator had learned and forgotten his long lessons." This criterion was not aggressive enough for the 1920's, with its galaxy of self-conscious experiments. As a sign of the changing times, *Homely Lilla* was published by the youthful firm of Harcourt Brace, an event which ended Herrick's ties with the old-line houses; but the technique of the novel did not venture beyond well-made fiction richer than the commonplace level of Howells, and it lacked the symbolic depths of Fitzgerald's *The Great Gatsby*. Also, unlike that of Gatsby, Lilla's history unrolled in the forthright sequence that suited older tastes. The disciplined tone and informal style, however, and especially the view of human nature belonged to the postwar spirit. Joseph Wood Krutch, then a young but already persuasive critic, proclaimed for *Homely Lilla* a "new grasp on fundamental things" and a matching honesty of treatment, evident from comparing the death scene of Adelle Clark's son with the opening chapters in which Lilla finds her father mangled on a power saw.[9]

From this gory (and perhaps symbolic) end to her childhood, Lilla is carried into middle age. For a few more years she endures her narrow mother in a relationship that escapes simple formulas. She drifts into teaching, allowing Herrick to rake the officialdom of public education again; indeed, she marries the principal of a high school, a nasty careerist who evolves plausibly into a would-be politician and who keeps trying to force his wife into his mold. Having eased up on moral dogmatism, Herrick had lately come to admire the Jamesian "novel of character" built on "psychological adventures, internal adventures." But he continued to hold, as he had asserted in "The Technique of the Novel" (1908), that "characters that have no outer life are shadowy, vague."

Lilla is substantial both inwardly and outwardly; she is stable emotionally yet beset by problems, especially those caused by her husband's clawing progress. While stable, she is reflective and, more haltingly than a Willa Cather heroine, learns from experience, thereby satisfying Herrick's cherished principle that a novel should trace "growth of personality." However, he had so relaxed his demands for purity of soul as to observe in the *Nation* of September 18, 1920, that "man—or woman—viewed solely as a sinning human animal is lacking in sustained interest" and scants the "whole host of human impulses." Instinctively broader than churchly rules of right and wrong, Lilla grows in sensitivity and timbre despite or sometimes because of her missteps.

One misstep is clearly a sin in the world's eyes. Giving the novel a brief *succès de scandale*, she has sexual intercourse when eighteen; having acted out of curiosity and impulse, she does not try to pretend afterward that she had been in love. Frightened and confused, she then retreats into twenty years of married respectability. But, when seen last, she has slept with a neighboring rancher—this time acting openheartedly in tune with the fenceless West. Herrick's notebook for 1910—11 held a brief essay on "Sexual Morality" contending that intercourse should be judged only by the intentions and needs of the two parties; *Homely Lilla* worked up to dramatizing this point honestly. As the name of John Slawn suggests, the rancher is made inelegant and prosaic with no apologies to the proper-minded or pleas for special privileges. More healthily emancipated than any flapper, Lilla hides nothing from the husband who reappears, now a failure seeking a haven. Experience has taught her that the "way to the spirit at some point leads through the senses, that sex enriches love just as love elevates sex."[10]

Lilla arrives at this discovery only by overcoming much poor guidance. Her mother, who is credited with a New England girlhood in a touch surely costing Herrick a pang rather than exploiting a current cliché, approaches even married sex with repugnance. Her peers in high school are ridden by furtiveness, perplexity, and guilt. Attracted subconsciously by her warmth and spontaneity (which her mother derides as "homely"), her husband virtually regrets his gusts of passion and abhors having children. Eventually, he turns to a secretary who caters to his selfishness; when a scandal breaks, he sheds her coldly, while Lilla, moved by simple pity, rescues her from suicide. Jack Pemberton, that unseducible paragon of *The Real World* who can decide that an embezzling brother might as well go to prison, would have thought that Lilla needed his standards. Already dead, Randolph Bourne would have exulted because Lilla scorns the chance at self-denying redemption when her husband wants to retreat into her arms.

Reluctant though Herrick was to admit it, part of Lilla's courage sprang from Freudian ideas seeping into the American mind. He would never accept them ungrudgingly. His best reason for resisting was that the psychoanalytic system could become a set of preconceptions that blur the features of unique individuals. Nevertheless, he had started as early as *Together* to look for a chain of unconscious cause and effect and to face the multivalence of sexual malaise. In *Homely Lilla* these tendencies grew much clearer, though his study of psychology may have gone no deeper than Havelock Ellis. By then, he had the sophistication to give the wife an honest show at turning out as the better adjusted partner.

Sexually liberated heroines of the 1920's, like Brett Ashley of Hemingway's *The Sun Also Rises*, often appear as shallow as their ethereal opposites—and not only to the prudish. Lilla has depth because of her gathering tenacity and self-reliance which climax in a shoestring venture at ranching in Idaho. This vein of practicality draws its strength from a primal energy, from what Joseph Wood Krutch's review defined as an "almost Nietzschian . . . celebration of the triumph of vitality" and the "wills to life and happiness." Her energy wins out, more credibly than irresistibly, in what might seem a cut-rate version of a happy ending. But Krutch caught the intent to evoke a fundamental élan without glossing over the post-Versailles debacle. In an unpublished essay—"What the Public Wants" (1914)—Herrick, now without any undertones of faith-healing, had urged that "joy is a sounder principle of life than pain." If the post-Hiroshima mind can accept this principle, Lilla embodies it worthily.

Another reason for the warmth of *Homely Lilla* is that it best met his own advice that our novelists must show more of the "little people." While Lilla never sinks into the working millions of the cities, this novel was his first and last to explore no higher than the solid middle class; despite her husband's schemes for climbing, she has no contact with the social leaders of Chicago. Similarly, Herrick made effective use of a resentment bred by his old love for his father's brother. In a late memoir he protested, thinking of his farming uncle: "Why should all forms of physical labor, with its attendant sweat and smell be considered so degrading? " Fleeing from the neat but stifling suburbs, Lilla seeks the routine her father loved—muscle-stretching labor in the sun and rain with the pleasures of handling animals and coaxing the earth to produce; and labor she does with profit skimpy enough to puncture any dream of pastoral dabbling. (Ten years before, incidentally, Herrick had started shaping up a modest house and grounds in Maine.) For the addict of cities, Lilla exemplifies the broader lesson that struggle is good for man when it stresses creative rather than competitive goals.

In denying that the thrust of Herrick's fiction had been merely negative or sympathetic only to the talented, Newton Arvin saw a host of characters sustained by "unaffected humility, the love of a task for its own sake, homely incorruptibility, freedom from self-absorption, and the sense of solidarity with a family, a profession or a class."[11] This overstates the total case but fits Lilla perfectly, including her tacit kinship with the "little people" who trudge along in obscurity. The ruling temper of the 1920's, suspecting Victorian homiletics, shied away from such a heroine. If Lilla did look to the past, it was to the agrarian tradition, though her life also involved the latest issues through her husband, who acts out the rise of wartime hysteria with its snooping on the foreign-born and even the mildest dissenters, its pomposities, its superpatriots who wangled fat salaries on the home front instead of rushing into the trenches, and its air of carnival more than carnage. Still, the topical was subordinated in turn to Lilla's humble concerns, leaving the next novel *Waste* to prove that Herrick's concerns could still center on the health of American society.

V *Another Summing-Up*

One of Herrick's occasional book reviews had lately restated his belief that the "enduring" province of the "real novel" is "social history" because men cannot understand themselves apart from their times. *Waste* (1924) aimed to project what he had learned about society, particularly in the last ten years. Yet he also felt impelled to reaffirm his supramaterial side. In 1933 his answer to a request for a capsuled self-analysis declared that, while "education, training, and conviction" pulled him into the "realistic school," his art stubbornly kept "romantic and idealistic elements." *Waste* bore out this shading of emphasis, with its crammed and jarring narrative buoyed up by a quest for emotional richness as much as for a metaphysics. With no courting of suspense or loud climaxes, the chronological framework carries a design engineer from his Yankee boyhood into a cosmopolite middle age; his activities serve as an index to social and political history, since he manages to turn up for the major events like the Chicago Fair of 1893 or spend much of World War I in Washington; his recurring encounters with old friends, who have usually changed for the worse in the meantime, amplify the effect of corruption though he resists joining the pack. Facing up to the truth about his vapid mistress as the novel closes, he sedately foreshadows Jake Barnes of *The Sun Also Rises* (1926).

Waste won essentially admiring reviews from Krutch, Harry Hansen, Henry Seidel Canby, Lloyd Morris, and Allan Nevins. For the *New Republic*, from which much of the novel's politics came, Carl Van Doren praised its panoramic sweep and its dialectic between the engineer and the artist, the "man of action" and the dreamer; though finding *Waste* "less impassioned than intelligent," he asserted that Herrick "rises among his contemporaries like a rock, battered but unsubmerged, weathered but unbroken."[12] The panorama was again judged by a hero much like Herrick, and early chapters on Jarvis Thornton's childhood in Cambridge and Harvard education seemed to repeat several previous novels. Even this latest hero's name echoed that of Jarvis Thornton in *The Man Who Wins*, Thornton Jennings in *The Gospel of Freedom*, perhaps Jack Pemberton in *The Real World*, and—only in part, fittingly—principled but humble Steve Johnston in *Together*. However, his formative years had facets lacking for his prototypes; and Thornton's classmates at Harvard included crucial additions such as McKeon and Gerson, two poised disciples of making good in business. The enriched insight is neatly typified by silken Elsie of *The Real World*, who helps Jack to success yet fails at seducing him, and Leslie of *Waste*. Again a shining maiden at first, Leslie soon proves tinnily genteel, teases a still callow Thornton with sex play, later seduces him— literally—into marriage as an escape from shabby widowhood, and drains him of money.

The weaknesses of *Waste* do not, then, result from its working of old ground. In fact the episodes in Chicago, where Thornton struggles as a young engineer, pulse with the somber lure that city always held for Herrick. Quality falls off when the war looms up; therefore, Herrick apparently needed more time for absorption before he could do better than Thornton's mounting diatribes on the news as the action in *Waste* almost reaches the year of publication. Its closing bitterness should be suspected as more hortatory than nihilistic though Blake Nevius ranks the last fifty pages among the very best of Herrick in their "profoundly elegiac" loneliness and another critic finds it the pivotal novel of his career because for the first time "the sense of defeat in the quest defines both tone and paraphrasible content."[13] The years left would prove that Herrick held on to much of Lilla's stout resolution.

Except for the dogged, few readers will ponder Thornton's ideas to the end, or his loves. The last of them, Cynthia Lane, grows boring long before he gives up on her as another mirage in the search for a perfect union. In 1916, despite Herrick's anxiety over the war, his notes for "The Love Book" explored the "connection of Sex with Spirit" rather than "voluptuousness." This lofty approach explains why his novels never dipped toward prurience. If his thinking sometimes equated Life with Energy and then Energy with Sex (perhaps the rationale for "homely" Lilla's vitality), he always insisted that sexual drive must be etherealized. He excused his own amours as a brave campaign to find a bridge between the material and the spiritual and to prove with a robustness foreign to Emerson that the flesh can lead into transcendence. As gloomily as Hawthorne, Herrick suspected that to fail in loving a worthy woman is to fail crucially. But, betraying Herrick's own continued disappointments, Thornton's mistress—self-named as Gioa (or Joy) on his behalf yet prone to be bullied by her mother and foolishly loyal to a spoiled son—falls short of suggesting even an echo from the ideal realm.

Thornton's professional judgment is, happily, much sounder. In all of Herrick, Thornton is the closest approach to the artist as hero: he becomes an architect similar to Frank Lloyd Wright in his designs, especially for a project that recalls the Midway Gardens in Chicago. Yet, primarily an engineer, he plans shipyards and railroads with Herrick's respect for solid efficiency; he ends up teaching at a technological institute rather than at an academy of fine arts. As Van Wyck Brooks has indicated, Thornton now and then resembles Thorstein Veblen's ideal engineer who is dedicated to solutions uncompromised by the profit motive. He also resembles Veblen in detesting showy drones, the anarchy of laissez-faire, and the wasteland of shoddy luxuries that succeeded the crudeness of preindustrial towns. More fundamentally, Thornton, perceiving an interplay that defies simplistic remedies, makes the same fusion of cultural and economic criticism.

But *Waste* never mentions Veblen, and properly so. Its tone is more heated as well as more vitalistic than that indulged in by the saturnine economist, whom Herrick barely knew as a colleague in Chicago. A stronger influence came from Friedrich Nietzsche, who is cited when Thornton is advised that the creative man must shake off his parasites despite the chidings of stock sentiment or custom and that "each one of us has something to do, something to offer, some function to fill, and it is just weakness or timidity or stupidity that makes us refuse to perform our function" (142–43). Still, though Nietzsche would supply the epigraph for a later Herrick novel, Walter F. Taylor strikes closer to the center of *Waste* by arguing that Herrick thought like the New Humanists of the 1920's, with their dualism between Man and Nature and their stress on personal responsibility.

This agreement was essentially a case of parallel growth from the common breeding ground of Harvard. However, Herrick lacked the New Humanists' crucial hostility toward science; like the Puritan metaphysicians, he assumed that rationalism confirms the ethical laws underlying the universe. Also, the temper of Thornton's ethic—"chilled to the bone," said Krutch in the *Nation*, and "sustained only by an intellectual love of integrity"—suggests Jonathan Edwards, Puritan, more than Irving Babbitt, Humanist. Thornton once goes so far as to warn: "Detachment, poverty, suffering—these were the three rules of discipline that led the human spirit" (215). Nevertheless, he aspires toward Beauty rather than God; he keeps trying to capture Gioa through both the spirit and the flesh.

The sometimes diverging lines of *Waste* did have a center—an ethical theory ascendant on campuses of the 1890's and the early 1900's. Herrick knew it best from the writings of George Herbert Palmer, the hub of Harvard's department of philosophy and also a protective uncle with whom he corresponded for many years. Assuming moral law without insisting on a doctrinal God, Palmer advanced a system of self-realization or the fullest development of the senses and mind. This system made room for beauty and for culture as an institution as well as for mental rigor. Likewise, while praising the control of animal impulses and the virtues of asceticism, it allowed for temperate pleasures of the body and adventures in creativity. It rejected modern society wherever a high-minded course became impossible or talent was frustrated; it also rejected the competitive race whenever self-realization was impeded, as in Thornton's case. On the other hand, it encouraged social concern. Palmer's *Altruism* (1919) summed up the position that the individual fulfills himself best in two ways—by dedicated love for his fellow man (or woman, Herrick might add) and by building the good life for all. At the end of *Waste*, though embittered with society, Thornton joins a technological institute in order "to humanize it somehow." Dubious of succeeding, he still feels obliged to make an effort at service.

In going back to teaching, Thornton was affirming the special faith in education that ran through Palmer's ethics. Furthermore, none of Herrick's fictional heroes entirely gives up on current society. An introduction to Hawthorne's *Twice-Told Tales*, which he edited with a junior colleague in 1903, had asserted that most great artists pass through three stages: focus upon the "outward aspect of the world," allegory that reflects their inward course, and escape from "egotism" back to seeking the "hidden laws" of everyday surfaces. Correctly or not, Herrick would have accepted this as a diagram of his own career. Though continuing to chide individuals for laxity of will, he now believed that the milieu would deform them irresistibly unless concerted action demanded changes. He therefore kept searching for a political vehicle and in 1924 started an essay on "Why I Shall Vote for LaFollette." But commitment to any party of liberals was blocked by Herrick's hardened suspicion that they merely wanted to pass out fatter slices of a capitalist pie (*Waste*, 176–77).

Instead, he inched toward a vague and mild socialism, finally resolving his lifelong imbalance between radical criticism and feebly traditional solutions. In 1923, he wrote to Lovett that he was reading *The Decay of Capitalist Civilization* by the Fabian oracles, Sidney and Beatrice Webb. *Waste* pressed their case for a rationally planned economy by excoriating "property" as a "master passion" and by dramatizing its corrupting effects or, less often, its blind torrent. For once using sheer accident sardonically, Herrick has Thornton enriched by a freakish coup in the stock market. In other words, the brainless economy pensions an enemy for a career of further intransigence.

Lacking a minute blueprint for the future, Thornton usually details flaws in the status quo. His most cogent note decries the greedy and ugly waste of natural resources. Though much traveled, like his creator, Thornton also warns that the insensitivity to our natural setting, coupled with over-flowing wealth for some, has encouraged rootlessness and sterile mobility. This last insight, sharpening since *Together* and vitalizing for *One Woman's Life* and *Clark's Field*, outstripped most of Herrick's younger rivals, who still thought of travel in its nineteenth-century guise of education or else fancied they were escaping bourgeois ways by enjoying Paris. Even more piercing is the emphasis *Waste* puts on civil liberties by showing how harshly the superpatriots hounded the dissenters in wartime and afterward. In total result, Herrick's own thirty-year war on the chaotic yet dully standardized values of a business culture was brought stingingly up to date. Only the terser, more striking novels from the "lost" generation keep *Waste* from being better known as a massive protest against the tawdriness of the 1920's.

The generous acclaim that greeted the novel persuaded Herrick that his dissatisfactions with it were overblown. After his writing days were done, he picked it as his most important novel; it was not, however, his finest. The crowded canvas he admired was not his most effective scale, as his remaining fiction soon proved. And, when he became a social conscience, he often sounded too shrill; unsurprisingly, his estimate of society convinced best when it was implied, not trumpeted. Likewise, Alfred Kazin suggests that when Herrick pondered not the "grossness" of the business culture but its "sadness," "not its paraphernalia but its emptiness," he approached the "tragic sense that gives him his distinction."[14] His last fiction throbbed more quietly with the tragedies of Americans blinded by selfishness.

CHAPTER *5*

A Retreat Forward

Herrick's last years ran in opposing patterns. Only fifty-five when he resigned from his professorship in 1923, he had fifteen active years left; but he was ailing, mostly from variegated tensions, and seldom felt positively well. Eager to call someplace home, he decided that the secret lay in picking almost anyplace and investing it with his personality; yet, though fond of his house in Maine, he traveled as widely as the most rootless Americans. Some of his other contradictions were to his credit and to the gain of American literature. Bred to a conservative esthetic, he disliked most experimental writing of the 1920's; yet he kept flexible and reached fresh heights in his last novel. Committed to a stern and individualistic ethic, he was appalled by the mass vulgarity of the 1920's; yet he never gave up searching for the perfect mate or camerado. From the first, seemingly, a snobbish loner, he showed less and less sociability; yet he became a man of action after advancing in his last book what is in some basic ways the most democratic of all utopias, a utopia that looks backward only to foresee a perfect fraternity. All in all, his closing years were a tribute to man's restless searching for values.

This search was bolder in politics than literature, for his opinions on modern innovators in fiction often show how the mental arteries can harden. Proust bored him, Joyce struck him as pedantic and futile and *Ulysses* suggested "marsh gas."[1] And (to get the worst over with) *A Farewell to Arms* he dismissed as "mere garbage," adding in a second attack that it smelled of the "boudoir, the brothel, and the bar." Actually, most of his comments on Hemingway made better sense; furthermore, his outrage sprang from not only an exalted view of love but also a belief—perhaps cogent in the long run—that the "hard-boiled school" constricts the range of human emotions and interests. But, loftily ignoring him as a fellow novelist, Hemingway lashed back at the New Humanists as the faction behind Herrick.[2] If Hemingway read *The Healer*, he never bothered to record his judgment on its version of love and idealism in the north woods.

Meanwhile, Herrick, despite grumbling again about Dreiser's lack of "charm, beauty, significance" or the arid emptiness of Virginia Woolf, was recognizing that the era of Thackeray and Tolstoy had ended. If far short of the avant-garde, he had not regressed or even stood still. If too slowly, he was accepting fresh ways of seeing experience without moral dogmatics and of putting it down more effectively. Once a casual friend of Henry James, whom Herrick showed around Chicago in 1905 and visited at Lamb House in 1907, he had long persisted in finding James's content "negligible" and "feminine." His papers, however, hold warmly perceptive notes for a book on James. As an involuntary tribute some other notes, which refer to "dear old James," plotted a "Last Book" in which passengers on an ocean liner who take turns at eating with an ingénue compare their impressions—"appraising, savoring the young person in the light of the latest returns of information." In an implicit rejection of his usual pattern, Herrick asked: "Is that not the way we pick up most of our knowledge about persons? Only less systematically, less positively." A late, unpublished essay granted ungrudgingly that the experimental novels of the 1920's sprang from a "growing consciousness of the inadequacy of the merely objective report upon life."

Herrick's margin of flexibility saved him from the conservatism that makes the guardians of the "genteel tradition" look stunted today. Eager for the novel to hold its dignity as a window on values, he eventually welcomed Dreiserean Realism for deflating "at least among the more vigorous and adventurous minds of our time the prettiness and moral illusion of the prevailing types of literature." Lewis' *Main Street* was also welcomed as a cleansing force in spite of its smart-aleck breeziness that must have irritated him. More crucially, he had learned to perceive that the "overtones and adumbrations and imponderables," which "go so far to make the atmosphere of the mind," respond to the current situation of humanity and therefore always create fresh themes for the writer. His last ventures in fiction projected a new atmosphere measured by that spirit of testing all traditions which is the finest legacy of the 1920's.

I *A Final Cycle of Short Fiction*

A sensible review of his *Wanderings* (1925), a collection of four longish stories, pointed out a hybrid strangeness: their "manner" smacked a "little of the old school" while the "matter" was more modern, making them "neither hay nor grass to the present generation of book buyers." Actually the stories were conventional in method, with standard blocks of description and no break from routine sequence. Even in matter they resembled the common love story with much less ethical and social concern than Herrick usually showed. But the lovers were avowedly middle-aged: he had decided that only seasoned ardor plumbs beyond superficiality. More familiar with regrets than fulfillments, he had also decided that the fading of romance holds more interest than its burgeoning. In subtle effects, therefore, *Wanderings* defied the easy stereotypes. Henry Blake Fuller, once a fellow warrior, could appreciate its ironies, hailing them as a reproof to the "juvenile and the non-significant." Self-furloughed long ago from active service, Fuller could not help adding wearily in his review for the *New Republic* that its characters took "things hard—like middle-aged beginners at golf."

This gibe was unfair to at least one story, "The Adventures of Ti Chatte," which flows along with a bantering, delicate comedy that Herrick never surpassed. Its leading figure—a woman anthropologist clearly like Herrick's latest mistress, who weaved through his fiction from then on— wavers intriguingly between egotism and aplomb, between smug naïveté and the maturity of a grandmother (which she is). Her feline poise contrasts vividly with the uncombed and rank luxuriance of a tropical island. Many other touches drew on Herrick's recent traveling in the Caribbean, but he distanced them with a happy-go-lucky hero who is surely not a self-portrait, even an idealized one. Though this hero captures the alluring grandmother, she makes it clear that she intends no redemptive change of soul. The idealizing reader must face up to as unsentimental and uneventful a study of the serious romance that begins past forty as American literature holds.

Neither of two related stories is successful. In the better one, "The Stations of the Cross," the coolly self-centered heroine learns to love by nursing her graying suitor through a feverish delirium. She captures some of the fascination that Herrick found in his current mistress while the setting achieves a patina of tropical brooding. Yet "The Stations of the Cross" is superior only by contrast with "Magic," a relapse into lovers who pour out their hearts in such strained tropes that "homely" Lilla would guffaw. Their fustian obscures Herrick's probing of Amerindian culture, shown first by *Waste*, and of the feminists' pull toward a career as a sexless intellect. When last heard from, the love-goddess of "Magic," having renounced private ecstasies, is barnstorming for a friendlier policy toward the Soviet regime that had been born in the turmoil of the late war. But her political force was wasted on a year when Hemingway's Brett Ashley and Fitzgerald's Daisy Buchanan sported with more colorful problems.

The least promising of the four stories, "The Passions of Trotsky," a tribute to a beloved pet in the Herrick household, turned unpretentiousness into solid wares. A dog attuned to total loyalty yet frustrated into antisocial ways by several changes of masters is made a reproof to humans who, like the "flower-girl" of "Magic," can quickly "fill a facile heart with substitutes." The dog's name, a sly pun, encourages a political reading also. Though wealthy friends mistrust the narrator for holding that the United States has treated "miserable Russia" too harshly, he indicates no choice between Soviet factions. Rather, the narrator lets four-legged Trotsky, who typically gets into trouble by harassing a lapdog, test the role of not "belonging to the protected classes and behaving like other people—what you call conforming! " Restrained by its lowly hero, "The Passions of Trotsky" merely protests against the "safe, prudently ordered, tepid." Still this protest may explain why the canine cult has ignored a piece superior to most of those it anthologizes.

II *The Inevitable Academic Novel*

Defense by comparison is more urgent for *Chimes* (1926). If Herrick had the talent for a masterpiece, this novel of academica surely offered his best opportunity after thirty years as a teacher. That he fumbled it should be weighed against the fact that among thousands of college novels, none, except perhaps Bernard Malamud's *A New Life*, is even second-rate. So prominent in our society and so interwoven with its values, higher education has thus far eluded its own Dante or Balzac. In the parade of failures, most of them abysmal, *Chimes* looks better than when taken strictly on its merits though it struck Jacques Barzun, then an undergraduate, as "fascinating." Apparently he was not bothered by its spurning all pretense to a shaped narrative along a core of action, or even theme, and its again retracing the main trails of Herrick's career, starting in this case with his move to the Midwest. The only viable tension of the novel lies in the implicitly inside look at faculty life.

A humor magazine for undergraduates brushed off *Chimes* as "about college professors written by a college professor for college professors." This triple-damning went to the heart of the matter. As yet, no campus novel has encompassed both the students and the faculty without hurrahs for one side that suggest the "grudge" game closing a football season. (Parents, alumni, big donors, political vigilantes, the impinging milieu— these modifiers must wait until the basic predication is resolved.) Inevitably, even aside from his weakness for mirror-heroes, Herrick cleaved to a faculty perspective. The conflicting estimates on his ability in the classroom agree that he gave short shrift to most students; Vardis Fisher, more baldly autobiographical in his fiction than Herrick, must have a similar judgment of Herrick in mind when deriding a teacher of writing at the University of Chicago, who looked like the "father of Minerva": "This man had a great forehead and a grotesquely wide upper lip; drooping eyelids that gave to his intellectual face something sinister and chilling; and an aloofness of manner, of thought, that stood like a wall between him and his students. 'The last of the puritans,' Vridar heard a woman say. 'If he'd lived in the seventeenth century he and Milton would have been chums' (*We Are Betrayed*, 168)."

While Herrick was gracious sometimes toward the gifted or an appealing stray, he resented the hordes grimly working off their requirements in English. He quipped that the "spiritual rewards" of teaching are "often" (not always, note) "stage money." The undergraduates of Eureka University, jeered his spokesman in *Chimes*, took it for a "sort of superior day school where one performed the rites of knowledge for a few hours each day and the much more elaborate rites of sport and society the rest of the time, with some sort of 'good Job' at the far end of the vista" (137). The post-Versailles crop irritated him more specifically with their "jazz, bootleg gin and whiskey, sexual freedom, with a new note of scorn or frank indifference for the old commandments" (294). Yet *Chimes* went right on to discount this snap judgment as the "sour prejudice of age . . . for behind this noisy facade of the fraternity houses was the great mass of the student body, hungry and eager, poor rather than rich, seeking life." Arriving in 1893 just before a boom collapsed, Herrick soon grew aware that many students at the University of Chicago were barely making ends meet, often in odd or grimy ways; well traveled academically too, he later realized that it had attracted a uniquely earnest, motley, and talented breed. Unfortunately, *Chimes* could not flesh out these insights.

Anyway, every academic knows colleagues who dislike students on the whole and yet believe in a community of learning. In *Sometime* (1933), education was vital to Herrick's ideal society, where the "best university spirits of the old order would have felt at home" (104). Beneath his grumblings at the cyclical grind, respect for its aims had held firm; after more than twenty years of service, he insisted that his subdepartment taught writing with genuine éclat. Though no Billy Phelps, Clavercin of *Chimes* quietly sticks to the campus, groaning much less than Herrick about how teaching stifles his creativity. This grudging was, finally, the main source of Herrick's malaise—regret at the energy put into grading papers instead of a new novel. Much of the remaining source lay in the fact that lecturing in a classroom stamped him as an academic.

Fiercely loyal to cronies, Herrick never respected his colleagues as a type. In his first published fiction about the campus—"Mother Sims," a gasping farce for the *Saturday Evening Post* in 1900—a football hero easily wins a coquette away from the unmarried director of her graduate study. That same year, Herrick jotted down a working idea: "Essential impotence and second-rateness of an associate professor borne home in him when an opportunity comes . . . to do something in the world that requires nerve and involves chance. . . . The 'ready-to-wear'-air, the littleness." This synopsis was a harsh preview of "The Professor's Chance" (*Atlantic Monthly*, May, 1901), in which a middle-ranker who has yearned for a wider career draws back because of timidity, liking for a lazy-paced routine, and a mild taste for scholarship. Better than *Chimes* at catching the tone of a faculty home, the story avoids masochism. But it implies a respect for more venturesome souls and a deference toward the mover of large affairs.

Chimes jeered that typical academics lacked fire and passion, that their households had a "meagre, forlorn air . . . because of the feeble sap that flowed dully through the veins of men and women professionally dedicated to the intellectual life" (221); even their admirable cosmopolitanism could pale into a tendency "to sigh" for European retreats (104—5, 178—79). An ideal dean would recruit "hearty men, good livers and lovers" who detest "ascetic" wanness. This jeering smacked of that envy of missed glories that pulls at many teachers in our era of showy consumption. The faculty at Eureka coveted both the status and salaries that their friends enjoyed through a business career: "Each felt that in some way he had been trapped by an illusion . . . a dream of something that did not exist in America or if it had once existed faintly in the older colleges of the East had been choked by the rapid growth of national wealth" (105). Built around an economist who left Eureka to join an investment firm and dropped back to the campus to have his expensive habits admired, one of the deftest chapters in *Chimes* reflected alarmingly well the Wall Street estimate of stodgy professors. And when those at Eureka dabbled in wildcat stocks, they came to grief, as in fact Herrick's colleagues had. A short story, "The Rainbow-Chasers" (*Canadian Magazine*, December, 1914), similarly derided their clumsiness as investors.

Still, an academic who reviewed *Chimes* for the Chicago *Daily News*, and conceded that it satirized him personally, praised it for showing a thoughtful, coherent, and elevated purpose. Part of this purpose was after all resistance, already begun in *Waste*, against opening the campus to those business methods and values Herrick could admire elsewhere. He also mounted a constructive defense, with some winning examples, of the humanistic tradition. Early in the novel, Clavercin muses: "I have it—a university is to discover and teach the Art of Life." The seasoned Clavercin's musings are a shade humbler but just as aspiring: a university "was, it should be, the home of the human spirit, removed from the merely passing, the fluid, the accidental, the one withdrawn place of modern life where all the manifestations of humanity could be gathered in essence and—handed on! " (268).

Giving ground to the increasingly dominant group favoring service to the community, Clavercin offered a "conception of apartness and yet cooperation in the life of the day"—now a cliché in which the apartness is practically smothered. Yet, though Herrick's utopia would follow John Dewey's lead, final emphasis fell in *Chimes* on the virtues of aloofness: "Caravansaries of the human spirit—that was what universities were. Often fantastically employed, according to the necessities or the whims of the moment, but always preserving their indestructible, indefinable, inner purpose for the human spirit."

The humanistic drive of *Chimes* was too often missed in a cloud of rumor about its unspiritual targets. For once, Lovett did harm by later offering clues and charging that the novel had broken a promise not to muckrake the University of Chicago. He especially chided the handling of the first two presidents, "who had been generous" in giving Herrick "freedom and support for his career and defending him when some of the trustees were scandalized at his realism" (*All Our Years*, 97). About William Rainey Harper at least, Lovett was too touchy. Though faculties are notoriously ungrateful toward presidents who charm tycoons into opening their vaults, the portrayal in *Chimes*, quizzical at first, warmed as it deepened; and it ended on a chord of heroism as an ebullient builder dying of cancer struggled to honor all his sanguine promises. On many similar points, Chicago alumni overreacted, spurred by intramural gossip. As the former colleague reviewing it for the *Daily News* saw, *Chimes* applied to "any expanding American university"—of today as well as then.

Exploiting the founding stages of aptly named Eureka, *Chimes* kept its focus on policies rather than on the men entwined with them, on the fate of the university ideal rather than private feuds. In the last chapter, a cornerstone goes down for a College of Business Science, but its pushy genie is passed over for president of Eureka: the humanists lose one round but get at least a draw in the next, and the balance of power will apparently keep on shifting. As a related pattern, *Chimes* indicates how inexorably routine and tradition end the adventures of building anew. The latest president is "neither radical nor conservative," is "not brilliant but everybody respects him." For better and for worse, Eureka becomes more like its ivied elders: it is muffled by a consensus wary of sweeping change.

Within the dominating effect of an academic procession, many vivid faces emerge in varying lengths of exposure, not always well calculated. Staunchly antiquarian but tolerant of modern foibles, old Bayberry stands out along with the first president and a saintly maverick sketched from

Lovett. Clavercin, the author's voice, is too modest to count at faculty meetings; but he casts light on Jessica Mallory, scholarly psychologist and wife of a campus politico. Another variation on Herrick's mistress, she defies the mores to expand into an enigmatic individualist, superior to amenities and superbly rational yet somehow unfulfilled. Echoing Anderson's *Winesburg, Ohio*, Clavercin eventually warns her: "I suspect that all your life you have been searching for something lost, inside, something that would release you and let you live.... Most of us are engaged on that quest. Only you have tried to achieve with your mind— and have failed" (217). No one, we suspect, will trigger her into spontaneity. Clavercin cannot; and, when seen last as she coolly moves on to a risky flirtation, she is more of an undismayed puzzle than ever.

III *The End of Realism*

Under the improved name of Serena Massey, such a mistress also dominated her lovers in Herrick's last novel, *The End of Desire* (1932). Yet this final variation ranged so subtly and deeply that no breath of staleness intrudes. Aware that every friend would take Serena as Mrs. Elsie Clews Parsons, a well-known cultural anthropologist, Herrick again belabored publicly those who match a writer's acquaintances with his characters.[3] With a passing jab at an old colleague, John M. Manly, Herrick granted the harmlessness of such matching with authors long dead like Chaucer; but he complained that living novelists were forced into "complete anonymity" to escape the scandalmongers. Of course, this scolding did not forestall the buzz of whispers. From an olympian view, far more notoriety would have been welcome because *The End of Desire* deserves admirers of its simple yet subtle, brief yet resonating, unshowy yet polished chronicle of a maturely reflective man who comes to realize that his mistress has cooled toward him and also—the chilling wound in the heart—that she was never worthy of his devotion.

Though Herrick's friends grasped footing for fresh gossip in *The End of Desire*, its strength came from deep-seated attitudes long refined. For the *Atlantic Monthly* of October, 1903, a short story, with the same title as the novel, adumbrated its climax of attaining resigned, wry insight after a prolonged fever of striving. In rich tension with this quest for inner peace, Herrick had never given up the hope for a perfect love union though it was paling into a "never-to-be-achieved dream." At the age of sixty, he was still rhapsodizing about the "ceaseless pursuit of satisfying beauty and charm, the search for full realization through women of all the glowing possibility of life" within oneself. In a timeless paradox such fulfillment could arrive only through devotion to the beloved. Therefore, during *The End of Desire*, Abner Redfield, a clinical psychiatrist and a widower on the downward slope of middle age, caters to the needs of Serena despite many signs that she merely considers her own pleasures. This taste for self-abnegation may explain, incidentally, why Herrick held loyal friends in face of the strains he put on them.

A harvest of ripened insights averted a relapse into bathos. Since Redfield is the narrative window, a sad wisdom from his previous failures gives the lovers, who are both grandparents, an elegiac undertone rather than an air of paunchy fumblings at rapture. For her part, Serena's brisk sexuality and her disdain for "literary" gloss keep the physical side prominent, allowing Herrick to draw a convincing line between love and sex for the first time. Furthermore, he had gone beyond typing the New Woman as pampered and restless. Cued by younger novelists superior to any trace of Victorian mariolatry, he now thought in terms of female range and wiliness, of feline "grace, furtive determination, slyness—and cruelty."[4] This view partly revenged a winded and despairing Don Juan. Yet, escaping rebound into another cliché, Herrick projected Serena's daughter and Redfield's daughter-in-law as, in their unique ways, troubled souls who were confused, vulnerable, and far from catlike.

The End of Desire interpreted the "war between the sexes" so freshly as to become revisionist in its impact. Herrick's blurb for the dust jacket stressed his transposing of the "ancient" roles. A few years earlier, he had spoken tritely of the "search, the demand for variety in the male, the jealous desire to possess and absorb in the female." But perhaps because of Mrs. Parsons' private example or the tenor of her writings, Redfield is made the faithful partner while Serena, whose daughter correctly warns that his term of favor will last around three years, flatly defends being what Dreiser called a "varietist"; at the opposite pole from a wife genteely enduring the mate's lust, Serena meanwhile has her climaxes without worrying about his.

This transposition also reaches outside the bedroom: Redfield is the homemaker, the arranger, and the satellite while Serena gives her scholarship and her working hours firm precedence over caresses. Redfield, trying at first to build bridges toward a marriage but eventually moved by protective warmth, even ends up looking after a son and daughter whom Serena treats less tenderly than her career. Anyone who knows Herrick's "Hermaphrodites" (*Bookman*, July, 1929), which growled that the garbling of sexual roles threatened "sterility, extinction," keeps expecting a sign that Redfield has violated manly bounds. In a letter to the *New*

Republic Mabel Dodge Luhan derided him as a spineless "gigolo" and, while basically praising the novel, gibed at its "mumbling revolt of man as he disappears into the matriarchy" brought on by his passivity. But the readers less committed to D. H. Lawrence will perceive unfailing respect for Redfield. Tutored by an anthropologist who was a precursor of Margaret Mead, Herrick was receptive to the chance that human nature might develop so freely as to break the molds that sexual custom fixes; his ideal of love called only for a self-abnegating union, with no prescribed traits for either male or female. Nevertheless, readers cannot forget Redfield's sex: he is admirable as a human being but somewhat defeated as a male. Far from a flaw, this imbalance creates a mature groping between fact and potentiality.

In the broadest analysis, *The End of Desire* contrasts two temperaments complex enough to need no thesis or thorny plot for support. It limns more than two unique personalities, in fact, but the gripping conflict is theirs. Each has virtues and weaknesses and each has attractive depths, though Herrick ultimately despised Serena's egoism. Besides many small details, he intended a self-portrait in drawing Redfield as a "romantic" of the subspecies driven by an "irresistible impulse to search for gold and make it out of common substances" (224); like the great Gatsby, both characters were so determined to find their dream palpable that they attached it to unworthy objects. Yet Serena—tenacious, aggressive, analytic, imperturbable, never ingratiating—has qualities that raise her to the dignity of a "lioness." While Herrick fondly saw Redfield in his emotional mirror, he possessed enough of Serena's traits to project her engagingly.

No ambivalences sway the handling of Herrick's matured concern for social justice. Early in the novel, Redfield clashes with the elitism of Ralph, Serena's older son, the only offspring she respects. Redfield—after meeting the whole "tribe," handsomely kept by the proceeds of a monopoly safeguarded with payoffs to legislators—decides that their motto is "Each feller for himself." His mistress, he begins to realize, typifies a New England foreign to the merchant-saints of Herrick's early novels; she not so much twists as ignores the Puritan tradition. Impervious to the principle that wrongs must be righted at any cost, she smiles over the Sacco-Vanzetti case while Ralph consigns the "dagoes," guilty or not, to a quick death for the peace of society. Redfield also demurs warmly at the smugness with which the wealthy sip their brandy while defending prohibition as salutary for the lower classes. (A vivid chapter records a Coast Guard swoop and miss at a rum-runner.) Still, Herrick was thinking too carefully to find fault only with the wellborn. Redfield's divorced son thickens into a salesman of inflated stocks; he is eager to marry the coarse and empty sister of his boss and embrace the worst side of the 1920's.

The End of Desire drove close to the hard-eyed candidness Herrick had lately deplored in the younger novelists. Though he would have insisted that it eschews both cynicism and pornography, his old publisher, Macmillan, rejected it as "too frank." It discusses lesbians and weaves male homosexuality through a sizable episode, and nothing essential to Redfield's beddings with Serena is evaded. Their final break comes when he tries and fails to stop her from observing an orgy among natives on a Caribbean island, an orgy set down with as little repugnance as misleading glamor. *The End of Desire* stopped short of using the frankest four-letter words, but it ignored most other genteel taboos.

Besides sexual honesty, the novel showed other signs of a remarkable capacity for growth at the brink of old age. Like Caroline Gordon's "symbolic naturalism," it uses setting functionally, as in the ugly climax that occurs against lush tropical squalor. The characters run far deeper than Herrick's redemption-prone sinners or mouthy paragons; having realized with Jessica Mallory that "this is a psychological world," he now "looked for the concealed, the hidden cause" (*Chimes*, 107). His sensitivity to motives behind both the routine gesture and the crucial deed approaches the magisterial, and it is more than adequate to sustain concern over the slow death of a liaison in which voices or tempers are never raised. Exploiting the limits of a much shorter span of dramatic time than he usually needed, he elicits an unfaltering intensity from two of the most controlled, not repressed, intellectuals in fiction.

This quiet intensity meshes with a mastery of the tone, which remains muted, reflective, and softly ironic despite his fondness for exclamation points. Blake Nevius, who finds *The End of Desire* his "saddest" novel, sheds definitive light in concluding that it is "filled with a kind of wry but uncomplaining wisdom based on the acceptance of human frailty." Though Redfield borders on despair as he strides nearer the treachery he foresees, Herrick tagged the novel as tragicomic on the dust jacket. Its irony is not savage or cosmic, nor merely condescending. Its style, much closer to the idiomatic than even *Homely Lilla*—which is echoed subtly in the subplot around Redfield's first daughter-in-law—pulses with patient honesty unmarred by witticisms. All the irony rises from character and reasonable event, as when the younger Massey children turn to Redfield just as he is losing their mother's favor or when the death of Serena's husband impels him toward seeking marriage and thus starts the final break or when he contracts malaria from trying to protect Serena, who resents his help as the last assertive straw. In the face of such cause for bitterness, Redfield moves only toward sorrow over man's inability to shape an end deserving of his best means. But his creator soon attempted to shape a better mankind.

IV *A Flight to Utopia*

An unfashionable cameo, *The End of Desire* sold decently; but Herrick's public had pretty much forgotten him. Furthermore, 1932 was a poor year to bring out almost any book as the great depression tightened its grip. Still *Little Black Dog* (1931) might have sold better if its publisher had kept solvent and active, for its doting over an Italian Pomeranian hit its target squarely. Reviewing a similar effusion in the Portland (Maine) *Evening News* of November 8, 1930, Herrick sighed that the book fell into the "old egotistical trap of interpreting dog impulses as human ones." Though the preface of *Little Black Dog* promised to avoid this "humanizing," his own book insisted that dogs show the full measure of devotion. In *The End of Desire*, Redfield's dog has the very last, voiceless word as it proves its "gift" of "caring utterly."

Fittingly, Herrick's career marched on past this sentimental note. His last years, with stretches of worry about his health and income, sometimes seemed capable only of sour gloom. But private worries were often submerged by his still deepening watch over social problems. He followed the news, debated with anyone handy, tirelessly refined his opinions, and kept printing them in hopes of dissuading wrong ones. Realizing more sharply than ever where his opinions had started from, he wrote in a symposium for the leftist *Partisan Review and Anvil* of April, 1936: "For all the years of my conscious life I have believed in what used to be called, fondly if rather vaguely, 'the American tradition' . . . that is, a cultural base differing from that of all other peoples, due to the physical environment, racial inheritances, and historical development of the American people. . . . The determining characteristic of this Americanism was an exaggerated emphasis on the values of individuality, independence, self-assurance, adventurous experimentation." After World War I his faith suffered periods of despair; but, bred to the party of hope, he seldom stopped trying to return his country to the track of greatness.

The great crash on Wall Street made despair more plausible than ever. In 1931, Herrick agreed dourly with the many who now held that the United States had moved only downward since the Paris Peace Conference. His essay "America: The False Messiah," for a collection branded *Behold America*! and apparently meant as a sequel to Harold Stearns's famous inventory, *Civilization in the United States*, belabored the 1920's for their red-hunting, union-busting, sullen isolationism that ignored our dependence on world trade, suspicion of foreigners, pressures toward conformity, and unleashing of big-time advertising. While not everybody will agree that his indictment was sound, it had more of a reasonable than a cranky air; and it justified its bile with harsh facts. Mixing socially by incongruous choice with the wealthy, Herrick noted their fondness for the countries run by dictators, their rumblings that the United States needed a Mussolini; the Republican party, he decided, had "properly gathered up all the fascist elements in our citizenship." Yet, before the New Deal, he could not believe that the Democrats marched to a much more noble drummer. One of his liveliest pieces, "Mr. Maggot's Fortune"—a profile of his rise and fall as an investor—signed off from the profit system.

Defense of that system can rejoin that Herrick's fiercest barbs came during its nadir. Also, they hummed with an ascetic glee in the collapse of luxury; "America: The False Messiah" contended that the New World "needs adversity, at the present crisis of her destiny, far more than she needs prosperity, inflated or sound, to chasten, enlighten and restrain the national spirit." The ideal of Puritan stewardship shone through his contempt for the moral callousness of "our supposedly 'best people'," for their alacrity to defend peculators like Samuel Insull, around whose collapse he sketched an "allegory of a Great Utility Magnate and the ruin wrought by him and his agents." But he also invoked mordantly current ideals as when his assessment of Virginia Woolf, which scored her characters for lolling in "futility" on the "exertions of others," proclaimed that not only the "communist" believed her kind of society to be doomed.[5]

In fact, Herrick's hunger for a creed of hope had led him to learn more about Socialism, and his learning was encouraged by Lovett. Though Lovett finally ran afoul of the House Un-American Activities Committee after World War II, he never joined the Socialist, much less the Communist party. Neither did Herrick, but the option no longer seemed preposterous. In 1932, he campaigned privately for Norman Thomas, the Socialist candidate for the White House, and dared to think of taking to the stump. Exploring still further to the Left, he seriously weighed a bid from the Soviet Publishing House to visit Russia and spend his royalties from a translation of *Waste*, which had sold well. With "either onward or dissolution" for his motto, Herrick eventually dismissed the New Deal as "silly and ineffectual" and concluded that the world was painfully "trying to pass from the cave man's social ideals to some sort of cooperative, communistic, non-competitive impulse." While the riots of the 1890's had unsettled him, the wider violence of the 1930's merely confirmed his expectation of sweeping changes.

His radicalism made room for the proletarian school of literature and esthetics. Fledgling novelists, he hoped, would absorb its scorn of "art for art's sake" as well as of the "neurasthenic school of postwar decadents concerned mainly with gin, sex, and Freud." On the positive side, Herrick praised the level of its militant fiction and echoed its rhetoric by calling for a "literature of revolt, which by spreading conditions and ideas in popular form becomes an active reagent in the change of bourgeois-conditioned minds, that must first take place."[6] As thin-skinned as most novelists, he was surprisingly humble toward criticism from the Left. When Granville Hicks proclaimed that his fiction, while "liberal" in impact, was lacking in basic (that is, Marxist) analysis, Herrick assured Lovett that what *The Great Tradition* (1933) "says about me seems to me not only discriminating and just but quite generous, from the viewpoint of the younger generation."

Spurred to revaluate his political path, he decided in an unpublished essay that he had never turned into an active reformer because no "panacea" was convincing. While convinced now that capitalism must fall, he still saw "nothing in itself desirable in the collectivist form of society" and no personal nirvana in dedication to social justice. He would never learn to march in a mass parade. Intent on the uniqueness of the inner self and its irreplaceable chance at fulfillment, he spurned the tactic of seeking or promising immortality through martyrdom to some future abundance for all. He would go on judging any society, real or imaginary, by the "spiritual condition of human life," by the fiber of discrete personalities functioning in their own present. Also, though cheering on the proletarians with the tactical opportunism of a Lenin, Herrick always circled back to his "early faith in the American tradition, in the so-called democratic process." Just as faithful to the allied doctrine of progress and incurably hopeful about man's rationality, he predicted: "If our segment of humanity, with all of its inherited advantages, cannot find its way between the Scylla of fascism and the Charybdis of communism, another human society will, in time." His last book, *Sometime* (1933), tried to imagine what that society could be like and thereby to help make sure it arrived before too long.

Ending his career with a utopian romance had also a literary logic, which his working notes explained: "The idea of Utopia is basic in the human mind. In fact it is against this basic dream of the human spirit that every so-called realistic work of art is projected, an unconscious tribute to the existence of an ideal by which the actual has been measured and found wanting." Obviously, *Sometime* intended to plunge deeper into the good fight. Instead of retreating into fantasy, Herrick as a utopist joined the much smaller wing who believe that the ideal society can actually be achieved. He proved his faith by refusing to waste attention on time-shift gimmicks or to concoct a distracting saga about how the "iron heel" of capitalism was thrown off and by sticking to the routine side of still fallible individuals who are merely our best selves, not glitteringly better than ourselves.

From the outset, his novels had fitfully demonstrated what men could be, not just what they woefully were. Furthermore, his moral paragons often conquered or molded their immediate reality; the end of *A Life for a Life* urged that human nature itself is "plastic," at birth anyway; and it set the redeemed heroine to work with children. His most bitter fiction had never gone so far as to deny that men can be creatively free, and his coolness toward the Progressive mind did not resist its high estimate of man's potential. After World War I, breasting the ebb of liberalism, he started belaboring the conservatives who argue from "human nature being what it is"; and soon after the crash of 1929 he readied a formal lecture on "Human Nature As It Is—or Isn't! " Warning that almost no decision is more crucial than whether or not to believe in the promise of our species, he contended for the side of faith; indeed, he inclined toward holding that mankind, especially when spared misshaping pressures, has already earned that faith. The utopian order of *Sometime* both reshapes human nature and merely liberates it. His spokesman Felix delights in pointing out that technology had come near perfection in the old order, which was mainly inferior at encouraging instinct and reason toward their noblest heights.

The faith in plasticity can be traced back to George Herbert Palmer's case for "personal perfection" or "perpetual self-development" as the goal of self-realization, which could serve as the password in Herrick's utopia. Yet *Sometime* has a firmly modern ring, reminding us that William James taught him logic and philosophy at Harvard and, much more important, that John Dewey taught as his colleague at Chicago though no link was then evident except perhaps in the ending of *A Life for a Life*. Eventual borrowing is certain. His lecture on "The Idealistic Solution" (1924) declared: ". . . for anything fresh or helpful in my reasoning I am surely indebted to Mr. Dewey." Easily persuaded that "ours is a mobile, not a fixed condition, a developing, not a static state," he had studied Dewey's *Human Nature and Conduct* (1922) to absorb its case for a scientific method wary of dogmas and its rationale for evaluating morality by the effects of practice and for rebuilding the social mores. At many crucial turns, *Sometime* draws a pragmatist's cheerful workshop that stresses experiment, not the simplistic "laws" of progress that chill respect for most utopias.

To attract converts, the utopist must project at least some concrete advances. As eclectic as most blueprints of the future, *Sometime* lifted details from varied sources including H. G. Wells, whose famous *Outline of History* had helped to encourage Herrick in the early 1920's by showing him how far men have risen above savagery. This rise did not require, however, the cramping of physical urges. Herrick's earthly paradise, which took a more equalitarian line than the Englishman's, had the same liberated and liberating sexuality. In its "anarchy"—that is, highly local rule through gentle example—sex is left to the dictates of enlightened taste. Since Herrick had long ago started heeding the feminists and suffragettes, no double standard of behavior hampers the women, who enjoy at least token equality in all matters.

Only a few citizens of his utopia abuse their freedom, while the sated majority fret much less than before. Carried away like a Freudian efficiency expert, Herrick predicted that, when "humanity was no longer teased and tortured by sex obsessions and repressions," its output would step up dramatically; if nothing else, "much time was saved" when the "individual was no longer worried about his sex life" (73–78). Yet this Franklinesque arithmetic, ignoble for a former devotee of Eros, was overshadowed by the rapport between Felix and a woman who raised the Serena Massey type into nobility by gaining warmth without losing intellect. In any case, the family, dear to Progressive sociologists as the agency for training children in altruism, carried little weight. (Herrick's mother would have wept at how few of his heroines rear their children wisely.)

Sexual play still met one very firm limit: suspending the ideal of inner-directed "anarchy," the Public Hygiene Board of Control enforces a set of eugenic rules. In 1913, responsive to a wave of popular interest, Herrick had considered a "grim Eugenics novel, with title of *Pro Patria Mori*—the preservation of the race." Confirming Randolph Bourne's view that eugenics was partly a faddish holdover of Puritanism, "The Idealistic Solution" wished for a society that combined Thoreauvian simplicity and biological planning. Happily, eugenics is suspect today, though Herrick's lecture avoided the worst pitfall by calling not for a breed of *Übermensch* but a "superior sort of average citizen." Furthermore, though *Sometime* makes much of the pedigree needed for a permit to bear children and glowers at overpopulation (a danger far less pressing in the 1930's), it explicitly challenges racism. Over and again, it glories in the racial mixture of its paragons: their head sage, Felix, is half Greek and half African. For that matter, the once "despised and enslaved" Africa has both geographically and biologically fathered the new order.

This fact underlined Herrick's refusal to pattern his utopia on American virtues, much less let it evolve directly out of his milieu as Edward Bellamy had done. Herrick had never shared the Progressive delusion that the millennium lay just around some familiar corner. Daily surer about the decline of the West and forecasting history by apocalyptic guides like John Strachey's *The Coming Struggle for Power*, Herrick had *Sometime* regard the ice sheet that smothered our continent in 1941 as merely the coup de grace to a civilization rotten within and bled by huge wars. When Felix sadly lectures on our past, he stresses the hypocritical cruelty and greed in its origins; the party he leads to the North American continent in the year 2998 contrasts incessantly and dismayingly with that of Columbus. In what seemed a farewell to the American tradition but was a desperate attempt to shock it back into vitality, Felix castigated it for starting "at the wrong end of the human problem, with the *rights* of individuals and their property interests, not with the *minds* of these individuals and their obligations to each other" (282). Though committed to individualism, Herrick had discriminated early among its effects; by now, he detested its possessive, atomistic variety.

Eyeing the sins of the present as much as the glories of salvation, Herrick entered many narrower complaints against his times—urban chaos, cheap journalism, conspicuous waste, the worship of the machine. No longer bound by faculty ties, he flayed the Rockefeller family as typical of the millionaires who squeeze wage earners to the "very edge of existence" while pacifying them with the "paregoric" of some well-bruited charity (57). Hard enough on New York City, Felix dismisses Chicago as "always a kind of swamp, socially as well as physically"; his research in its annals uncovers only one fine spirit, Jane Addams—branded a "crank" by the opinion-makers of her day (91—93). Journalists of the same stripe had lured youth into a war to "save democracy" when "there was no such thing in their world and least of all . . . in the United States, and could not have been under the sway of 'robust individualism'," which forced "corrupt and ignorant" legislators to serve as "merely the agents of the powerful owners of property" (279). Felix nails down his critique by opposing any resettlement of our domain, fearing that its "sparkling and tonic" climate stimulates "reckless individualism."

The one relenting toward the New World could only further enrage its superpatriots. For forty-five years Herrick had treasured the warmth and directness of the peasants in Mexico; another visit during the winter of 1932, while he was finishing *Sometime*, confirmed his memories. In the meantime, he had observed the Navahoes; and *Waste* praised their rearing of children who tended to escape the tension between personal and community needs. *Sometime* offered both the American and Mexican Indians as models for making a sense of community practicable. Betraying that Herrick had wearied of a lifetime of introspection that pitted him against the moral universe, the party from utopia admired even more the

Indians' submergence of self into the immediate group and the local rhythms of nature.

Though intelligence wins top honors in the explorers' homeland where, Herrick's notes stated, the "Professor, so long a subject of ridicule . . . had become the Supreme Authority," Felix praises unstintingly the Indians' "simple" outlook that is immune to the "white man's creed of Holy Desire" and egoism (336–37), their "primitive, passionate unreasoned conviction of the reality and the significance" of life. Herrick could never stop holding the individual as primary, but *Sometime* conceded that a man might need help from society in realizing himself; moreover, it even opened the chance that enriching his identity might not serve all roads to fulfillment. Echoing D. H. Lawrence, perhaps merely by chance, Felix decides: "No, the best we can do for the old New World is to let it alone! If Columbus and his followers had never invaded its shores, who knows what miracles its Indian people might not have accomplished. They might have discovered Europe before it was too late and saved it from its wretched fate" (333). This was Edenic reversion with a true vengeance.

While Felix approves the visceral directness of primitives, he favors various other innovations, among them a "mental hygiene" program at home. And, while he belabors the old professions for their uselessness, his society creates some dispensable specialists. The silliest is easily the Bird Choir Master, who trains young birds to sing together; each large community also has a virtuoso of aromas that he broadcasts, sometimes in orchestrated patterns. Dreamers waver away from common balance, but some of these absurdities can be excused as attempts to gain concreteness or to suggest the texture of earthly salvation. Like many of his contemporaries, Herrick had concluded—tardily—that political dysfunction may misshape or starve a culture and, conversely, that cultural poverty may demand concerted public action.[7] But he had the wisdom to pull up short of painting a stasis that would repel those who enjoy a hurly-burly world. True to the pragmatists' respect for the open-ended process, Felix insists that the new order will continue to evolve and halfheartedly concedes some flaws.

As the crowning rebuff to dogmatism, Felix argues that the Indians of Central America must be "let alone . . . to work out their own dream of life," without "our technical efficiency and mastery of nature," if only because "it is *their* dream" (337). Though hinting that the primitive and the intellectual styles may find a higher fusion some day, as they have partly done in the hybrid Felix, Herrick had embraced the possibility of there being more than one right way to happiness. This tolerance helps to prove that *Sometime* drew more on love than on niggling hate, that it meant to cheer man upward rather than crush him with contempt for his failures. Transmuting Herrick's religious fervor into wholly secular terms, it pulses with a quiet but venturesome confidence symbolized by the flying ships so commonplace in Felix's epoch, which neither wallows in gadgetry nor spurns the machine. For his own epoch Herrick praised the "impulse to fly" as attesting to the "great human urge for trying the unknown . . . for meeting new situations and new perils, for becoming something other than the patterned creature of inheritance." Such courage surely earned the right to dream of self-disciplined yet creative paragons who would redeem society even while being helped by it. Such courage gave *Sometime* a tone that its publisher described privately as "wise, humorful, serene."

V *Climax in the Real World*

In 1935, Herrick acted on his courage by beginning a fresh career in the Virgin Islands as government secretary, a position more imposing than its title. According to Nevius, he functioned as "combined Secretary of State, Education, and Labor" with "several minor portfolios" besides. Yet, as he fulfilled his varied duties well, he was quietly smug over coping with them as capably as the businessmen who condescend to intellectuals and artists. The day after his death, Harold Ickes jotted in a secret diary: "I was reluctant to appoint Herrick at first because I doubted his ability for this job, but he has performed wonderfully and his loss will be severely felt. Although a man of great personal dignity, he was a real democrat at heart and he had a feeling of sympathy for, and understanding of, the Negroes on the Islands."

This tribute recalls why Ickes' top adviser in the matter had urged Herrick's appointment. In the 1920's Herrick's travels had crisscrossed the Caribbean islands, which inevitably became grist for his fiction. Of greater interest to his political friends, two essays for the *Nation* (June 11 and 18, 1924) had rated both British and French colonial policy as more humanely realistic than ours. Three years later, his long article in the New York *World* called for pulling the Marines out of Haiti because so many were prone to racism; more constructively, in the *New Republic* (January 30, 1929), he advocated sending out "tolerant and sympathetic" experts "who do not classify humanity simply according to color" or lean toward using force. Recent history has vindicated his approach.

Herrick did not relapse into racism or paternalism when put to the practical test. In the relativistic vein of Felix, he opposed making the Virgin Islanders into "Americans from the point of view of Harlem"; he therefore advised tailoring any program to fit their traditions and local setting. At his worst, he now and then became dictatorial in his day-to-day routine, apologizing to Lovett: "I am more of an anarchist than ever since this experience of Government as Is, yet I rule here with a pretty firm hand, that is *ad hoc*, which is what the environment calls for." While usually siding with labor against the landowners, he clashed once with the American Civil Liberties Union—which had enjoyed his support at home during the 1920's. Increasingly fragile in health and therefore too peevish for an administrator, he still left most islanders convinced of his competence and goodwill.

After gloating that four years as government secretary had loaded him with fresh material, he never got around to using it. *Sometime* was his last major piece of writing. In the 1930's, a single sheet of ideas for "This Mad World" despaired, like Mark Twain's "great dark" items, of finding ultimate reason. Yet, again like Twain, Herrick could publicly beat the drums of hope until his death in 1938. Fittingly, his last printed words came in "Mark Twain and the American Tradition," the text of a lecture given at the University of Puerto Rico in 1935, which divided American literature into two patterns, the imported and the indigenous; and, while classing his work under the first, he declared gallantly that the second was "much the more important." Just as gallantly Herrick defended our political heritage, in terms straight out of Thomas Jefferson, and he hoped—in spite of Felix—that we "may be the people first to discover the way into the new life, the new conceptions of evolving personality." Herrick died a better democrat than he had been born. He had looked backward only to gain sounder footing for the next step forward.

CHAPTER 6

Conclusions

In our age of rigoristic criticism, the great writers are scolded frequently. One critic after another indicates how much better Flaubert's *Madame Bovary* or O'Neill's *Mourning Becomes Electra* would be if he could have revised it. But the ability to create has always fallen short of the ability to conjecture the perfect work. Furthermore, art forever transcends the most searching analyses. Henry James put this last point more humbly by warning that no theorizing can triumph over the test of whether the sensitive reader does or does not like a novel.

Herrick was fully willing to accept this test. In his declining years, he once spurned a request for biographical details by insisting that the novelist must be judged through his work.[1] Today Herrick has still greater need of an audience willing to give him a chance rather than biographers who plumb or weigh his private motives. More moral than esthetic or demonic in his drive, he undoubtedly turned to writing as a career in order to escape the business world, to further the self-realization central to his ethic, and to find a personal immortality to replace the fading Puritan heaven. But he also had a deep hunger to comprehend the specific culture thrust upon him. All in all, his motives require no apology; but a lasting reputation cannot rest on such grounds.

Since neglect threatens Herrick's entire output, there is little use in pounding away at his faults. Like most novelists bred in the nineteenth century, he wrote too copiously without enough revision, sometimes almost plagiarizing himself; his characters too easily fall into the hollow rhetoric and melodrama that have plagued fiction from the first; he thought too much in terms of plot, exploiting coincidence to keep his action complex and often ending his novels before 1914 with a moral conversion that sways only the sentimentalist. The "structures of his novels, particularly their resolutions, are too often dictated by his determination to prove that a way of salvation exists"; they are most satisfying when the "protagonist is irredeemable."[2] As his most serious failing in technique, he never really pondered what a novel is and what it might be. Eventually, he grew dubious of "trying to squeeze flowers into set forms"; yet his one published experiment, the fervid allegory of *A Life for a Life*, looked backward. At best, he finally learned, from his younger contemporaries, to depend more on symbolic economy and to shed the oracular, intrusive persona of the Victorians.

While technique is ultimately another facet of insight, conventional method can, as in the hands of Anthony Trollope, build a major fictional world. Herrick at times seemed to articulate only a private quarrel with life. This narrowness sprang from ethical urgencies that were too harsh on the imperfect and too shrill when a reformed sinner had a vision of grace. Still more repellingly, they made Herrick too austere in preaching "integrity" with a "profound" yet "bleak consistency," with an "almost mystical rigor," with "intelligence and conscience" rather than compassion.[3] Or, as another mostly favorable critic has objected, in his "early work the act was more important than the human being who committed it. Later the balance was adjusted, but . . . a really broad spirit of toleration, that bears with human frailties even in their pettiness, is lacking. The sharp edges of Herrick's will everywhere cut into the warm flesh of his world."[4] Only *One Woman's Life*, *Homely Lilla*, and *The End of Desire* resounded with the degree of forgiving empathy that great fiction shows. As in his private relationships, Herrick asked too much from his characters, who strain at satisfying both their conscience and the hunger of others for rapport. In short, he made almost unbearable demands on the individual.

The handiest comparison involves Howells and Dreiser. In tolerance toward a variety of sinners, Herrick may surpass the kindly but sedate "dean" of Realism. However, he fares badly when measured against Dreiser's brooding communion with the weak and confused: "Where the earlier writer admonished, appealed to better nature, insisted on an exercise of self-respect and self-restraint, Dreiser simply 'understands,' with a limitless human sympathy. Where Herrick sees the individual only in relation to society, as a vessel of duties and responsibilities towards a whole, Dreiser has only the frail piece of humanity before him, placed in a world of savage instincts and force."[5]

Conceding the understandable error of labeling Herrick as clearly "earlier" (he was born merely three years before Dreiser), the one worthwhile rebuttal is that his emphasis on duty and will had its own advantages. Though we respond most deeply to the novels that cherish a Hester Prynne, an Ishmael, or a Huck Finn, Herrick's more cerebral scale of values created characters who at least court admiration, who challenge us to reason through to disciplined insight.

If Herrick is to endure in American literature, it is as Dreiser's antithesis—as an educated intelligence. In *Chimes* he said of Jessica Mallory that she "could fight . . . for reason against unreason, but not . . . for the little, the weak, the down-trodden. The submerged did not appeal to her" (244).

This statement usually applied to himself. Though his social conscience kept expanding, his best subject was the reflective individual struggling with his ideals. Controlled intellectuality is rare in our novels; we have preferred almost any other quality—and even Herrick, like Emerson, ached to feel more passion. But he spoke far better to the mind than the heart, aroused the superego far better than the nerve ends. In the broadest perspective, he typifies the fate of an older individualism, wistfully recalling Puritan heroics by contending with an age that would narrow it to material goals or subvert it for profit. His faith in an inner-directed, naturally reasonable and self-improving mankind refused to settle for the "hard sell" as its destiny.

Because Herrick tested ethics against the market place, it is tempting to defend him as a social historian. Carefully defined, that role did appeal to him. Still, the commonplace made vital, as in Silas Lapham's crisis over whether to wear gloves out to dinner, seldom dominates the pages of Herrick, who was too righteous about others' extravagance in clothing and too insecure about his own tailoring to reproduce personal surfaces with affectionate irony. Anyone with an appetite for the incidentals of life in his day can feed as satisfyingly on other novelists, for the documentary value of Herrick's fiction lies rather in its firm-backed analysis of such vital segments of his society as its women and its most dignified professions.

Later nineteenth-century novelists had virtually made their treatment of women a touchstone for originality, and Herrick therefore inherited a formidable tradition. Some critics see it as reaching its pinnacle in Henry James, with subsiding peaks in Edith Wharton and Virginia Woolf. But Herrick created a striking gallery often bound closer to coarse reality than James's heroines. At least—to pitch our comparison less ambitiously— Herrick probed far beyond current sentimentalism, as Mark Twain did not, and beyond the patronizing banter of Howells' variations on Mrs. Basil March. A philanderer in private, Herrick was too knowledgeably involved to rest with easy condescension, much less with the savage war of caricature preferred by some males. His women are, regularly, believable as human beings.

To be so means that they range in many directions. It also means that some have superior personalities; they are shrewd but also warm, committed to ideals but also realistic about dealing with an imperfect present. The male chauvinists can smugly deplore Milly Ridge, if not blinded by her charm; but they must respect "homely" Lilla. Furthermore, Serena Massey is awesome as a razor-edged egotist who nevertheless dignifies the type of poised and competent women that were putting their new equality into practice. Notably emancipated from naïveté, they both repel and attract the male while competing in the modern professions or at least searching for a fuller role.

Herrick also cleared rich perspectives on the well-educated man seeking a career in a shifting world (with his problems often complicated by a wife who schemes for status). Architects, engineers, attorneys, editors, and physicians—the earliest galaxy of "professional" men in our fiction—cast about desperately for a calling that is productive and challenging, respected by others yet inner-directed. Carlyle had already questioned the savor of making cash profits the only criterion, and Thoreau had rejected most employment as frivolous or demeaning. But, anticipating Veblen, Herrick was among the first to pose the more pointed question whether the strong-willed entrepreneurs rushing corporate business into dominance would let the trained experts whom they were paying insist on loyalty to self-development and an integrity beyond dividends.

Posed more generally, one of Herrick's major contributions was to confront the latest gospel of success. He did so not merely from his Puritan sense of responsibility but also from commitment to the American tradition. Recurrently aware this tradition had a democratic base, he worried about the "common lot" or the spiritual dangers of rising above it. As for practical democracy, he warned that monopolists capable of dictating to governors and congressmen had negated the power of the ethically strenuous voter. *The Memoirs of an American Citizen* cut down to the harsh bones of a rags-to-overflowing-riches career in which finance inevitably meshes with low and high politics. Herrick cut deeper still. Even his Van Harrington suffers twinges of bewilderment, of hunger for approval from the best instincts of himself and others. Herrick insistently questioned whether, given the finer side of that human nature so often cited to discourage the utopian or reformer, the realm of physical fact can satisfy those crises of conscience or pampered luxury when the urges of the spirit reassert their strength. Without discounting the pull of materialism, he always kept its tragic insufficiency in view.

Still, unwittingly gestating one of the most democratic of utopias, he always came back to the more pointed protest that the American dream had promised to breed paragons of sensibility and purpose. Refusing to settle for Lucky Jim solutions or to counsel asceticism for the starving, he measured the business world by its spiritual demands on its would-be masters as well as on its servants. He has been accused of compromising sometimes, of letting his heroes make a truce with the profit system after all, yet this was further proof of his honesty. Like Howard Sommers in *The Web of Life*, he soberly conceded that even the rebel can get hungry and conform for the moment, however out of ethical joint that moment may be. Perfect formulas for integrity in a huckstering society are still as scarce as Herrick led his readers to expect.

In other words, Herrick tried hard to see how life actually works—as good a brief definition of the Realistic program as we still have after much refinement of terms. Better attuned to ideas than the characters who embody them in his fiction, he had the Realist's full enmity toward the false lights that men follow or pretend to follow. He particularly attacked the illusion of unbounded liberty, not denying, like the Naturalists, that free will exists, but doubting whether his contemporaries understood it or knew what to do with any degree of it. He also deflated some lesser illusions about the naïveté of Columbia's maidens, the sleek nirvana of wealth, and the permanence of lovers' ecstasies. At his best, if too seldom, such truth-telling merged gracefully into irony, into the self-condemning apologia of a cheerful Van Harrington or the gay astringency of *One Woman's Life* or the sardonic reversals of *Clark's Field* or the almost tragic undertone of *The End of Desire*.

In literary histories Herrick usually appears with the first wave of the "Chicago School," a reasonable and helpful grouping. But from the outset his frame of reference reached beyond Chicago, and his demonstrated sense of place was his weakest side as a Realist. Tending to regard the Midwest as "elementary" rather than "elemental," he could never fulfill his advice to the regionalists that their chosen locality must become a "solid world of the first magnitude in itself" as if it were the "literary centre" of the universe.[6] His achievement belongs not to any provincial or tangential movement but to the main line of Realism. Surprisingly tacit about his literary forerunners, he vowed to extend the thrust of the latest European masters like Maupassant. In practice, his fiction also showed increasingly how the legacy of Howells could be tempered into a tougher, keener instrument for dissecting illusions.

It is heartening that Herrick did keep developing since our novelists too seldom do so after their first mature work. Publishing for nearly forty years, he never rebounded for long into nostalgia or even hauteur; in 1914, already faced with a shrinking audience, he insisted that the novelist should address not a "few intellectual and theoretical aristocrats" but the "great majority."[7] Nor was this a prelude to courting a lowbrow market. Oscar Cargill has wondered at Herrick's steely determination "not to write down" to the public and at his "amazing lack of fictional amenities." Patrons of serious fiction formed his chief support though less richly than he would have enjoyed and though, like any self-respecting artist, he felt that he gave much more value than he received. Today the need is for new readers to judge whether he was right.

Notes and References

Wherever convenient, materials cited are indicated in the main text. Since few of Herrick's novels have been reprinted, I use first editions as they are still, in general, the most available. Herrick materials cited in the text but not listed in the Bibliography are unpublished; they can be seen in the Robert Herrick Papers held by the University of Chicago Library; Blake Nevius informs me that a vital section of George Herbert Palmer's correspondence in the 1890's has lately become available through the Houghton Library of Harvard University. Herrick was a less than polished typist and a less than perfect speller; he was capable of "naval" for "navel" and "peeled" for "pealed"; I have silently corrected obvious misspellings in unpublished materials.

Much of my biographical detail is based on Blake Nevius' truly excellent *Robert Herrick: The Development of a Novelist* (1962). I have used it more heavily than it was convenient to show by continuing citations. In critical interpretation Professor Nevius and I differ often. But I saw no need to note this in most cases, where his thinking nevertheless pushed mine further than it would have gone otherwise.

Preface

1. Letter dated September 28, 1908; now in Hamlin Garland Collection of the Library of the University of Southern California.
2. See Harald Nielsen, "The Novels of Herrick," *Poet-Lore*, XIX (Autumn, 1908), 337–63.
3. C. C. Baldwin, *The Men Who Make Our Novels* (New York, rev. ed., 1924), p. 244.
4. H. Lüdeke, "Robert Herrick, Novelist of American Democracy," *English Studies*, XVIII (April, 1936), 57.
5. Grant C. Knight, *The Strenuous Age in American Literature* (Chapel Hill, N. C., 1954), p. 228.
6. Arvin, "Homage to Robert Herrick," *New Republic*, LXXXII (March 6, 1935), 93.

Chapter One

1. Herrick Papers, "First Memories," pp. 46–47.
2. Herrick, "The American Way," *Partisan Review and Anvil*, III (April, 1936), 7.

3. Herrick, "New England and the Novel," *Nation*, CXI (September 18, 1920), 323.

4. Herrick Papers, "First Memories," p. 30.

5. Herrick, "The University of Chicago," *Scribner's Magazine*, XVIII (October, 1895), 417.

6. The fullest, most systematic discussion of Herrick's undergraduate stories is in Grace Stuart Nutley, "The Social Criticism of Robert Herrick," New York University, doctoral dissertation, 1945.

7. Herrick repeats the formula in his preface to an edition of *Silas Marner* in 1895; see also his notes (dated 1898) for English VI, taught at the University of Chicago.

8. Anon., *Book News* (Philadelphia), April, 1897.

9. See Chapter II of George M. Spangler, "The Theme of Salvation in the Novels of Robert Herrick," University of California at Berkeley, doctoral dissertation, 1965.

10. Howells, "American Letter, Chicago in Fiction," *Literature*, II (July 2, 1898), 758–59.

Chapter Two

1. Herrick, "That Sort of American," *New Republic*, XXII (March 21, 1920), 153.

2. Quoted in Daniel Aaron's introduction to a reprinting of *The Memoirs of an American Citizen* by Harvard University Press (1963).

3. Swinburne Hale, "Mr. Robert Herrick and His Realism," *Harvard Monthly*, XXXVI (May, 1903), 105–11. Almost as laudatory is Nielsen, "The Novels of Herrick," pp. 361–62.

4. Blake Nevius, *Robert Herrick* (Berkeley and Los Angeles, 1962), p. 121.

5. Knight, *The Strenuous Age in American Literature*, p. 94, f.n. 30. This claim may hold for civilian dialogue, though in the heat of battle two Confederate soldiers in DeForest's *Miss Ravenel's Conversion* (1867) are allowed fullness with the same epithet.

6. Spangler, "The Theme of Salvation in the Novels of Robert Herrick," p. 62.

7. Oscar Cargill, *Intellectual America* (New York, 1941), p. 585.

8. Howells, "The Novels of Robert Herrick," *North American Review*, CLXXXIX (June, 1909), 817.

9. Lüdeke, "Robert Herrick, Novelist of American Democracy," p. 53.

10. Quoted in Nevius, p. 157.

11. Mildred Howells, ed., *Life in Letters of William Dean Howells* (Garden City, New York, 1928), II, 230.

Chapter Three

1. Identification of these editorials—not always unquestionable—depends on clippings in the Herrick Papers.

2. Herrick, "An Author's Models," *Literary Review*, III (August 18, 1923), 905—6.

3. Spangler, "The Theme of Salvation in the Novels of Robert Herrick," p. 32.

4. Kenneth S. Lynn, *The Dream of Success* (Boston, 1955), pp. 231—33.

5. Nevius, p. 180.

6. Herrick, "The Booze Age," *New Republic*, LXVIII (October 7, 1931), 213—a defense of Upton Sinclair.

7. Nevius, p. 225; Nevius is especially informative on *Together*.

8. Robert A. Holland, "*Together*: A Nietzschean Novel," *Sewanee Review*, XVI (October, 1908), 501.

9. Quoted in Baldwin, *The Men Who Make Our Novels*, p. 244.

10. Nevius, p. 200.

11. Herrick Papers, "The Realistic Picture," p. 7.

12. Herrick Papers, "The Romantic Picture."

13. *Ibid*.

14. Nutley, "The Social Criticism of Robert Herrick," p. 110; Lovett, *All Our Years* (New York, 1948), p. 96.

15. Herrick, "The American Novel," *Yale Review*, N.S., III (April, 1914), 426.

Chapter Four

1. Herrick, "The Background of the American Novel," *Yale Review*, N.S., III (January, 1914), 215.

2. Herrick, "A Late Victorian in Ohio," *New Republic*, II (March 13, 1915), 152, and "An Author's Models," *Literary Review*, III (August 18, 1923), 905—6.

3. Bourne, "Theodore Dreiser," *New Republic*, II (April 17, 1915), Part II, 7—8.

4. Spangler, "The Theme of Salvation ir the Novels of Robert Herrick," p. 129.

5. Quoted in Nevius, p. 242.

6. Introduction to Ludovic Halévy, *Abbé Constantin and A Marriage for Love* (New York, 1902).

7. Quoted in part by Nevius, p. 262.

8. Herrick, "The War and Ourselves," *Survey*, LII (August 1, 1924), 493—95.

9. Krutch, "Mr. Herrick's Return," *Nation*, CXVI (February 14, 1923), 190.

10. Spangler, p. 178.

11. Herrick, "Homage to Robert Herrick," p. 95.

12. Van Doren, "Forty Years in the Wilderness," *New Republic*, XXVIII (April 23, 1924), 235. Richard J. Thompson, "Themes and Tendencies in the Social Criticism of Robert Herrick," State University of

New York at Buffalo, 1964, asserts (p. 208): "It is known by older New Englanders, though not recorded, that Herrick's books were put under a non-formal ban by New England librarians because of his anti-war sentiments from about the date of *Homely Lilla* on. The hostility of the American Legion toward Herrick is also known."

13. Spangler, Chap. VI, "Final Defeat."

14. Kazin, "Three Pioneer Realists," *Saturday Review of Literature*, XX (July 8, 1939), 15.

Chapter Five

1. Nevius, p. 278.

2. John A. Yunck, "The Natural History of a Dead Quarrel: Hemingway and the Humanists," *South Atlantic Quarterly*, LXII (Winter, 1963), 32–36.

3. Herrick, "The Necessity of Anonymity," *Saturday Review of Literature*, VII (June 6, 1931), 886. On Mrs. Parsons, see Henry F. May, *The End of American Innocence* (New York, 1959), p. 309.

4. Herrick, "A Feline World," *Bookman*, LXIX (March, 1929), 6.

5. Herrick, "The Works of Mrs. Woolf," *Saturday Review of Literature*, VIII (December 5, 1931), 346.

6. Herrick, "Writers in the Jungle," *New Republic*, LXXX (October 17, 1934), 259–61.

7. Christopher Lasch, *The New Radicalism in America* (New York, 1965), p. 163.

Chapter Six

1. Stanley J. Kunitz, ed., *Authors Today and Yesterday* (New York, 1933), pp. 310–12.

2. Spangler, "The Theme of Salvation in the Novels of Robert Herrick," p. 248.

3. Carl Van Doren, *The American Novel, 1789–1939* (New York, 1940), p. 244.

4. Lüdeke, "Robert Herrick, Novelist of American Democracy," p. 56.

5. *Ibid.*, pp. 56–57.

6. Herrick, "A Late Victorian in Ohio," *New Republic*, II (March 13, 1915), 152.

7. Chicago *Tribune*, April 12, 1914.

Selected Bibliography

PRIMARY SOURCES
(in chronological order)

1. Books

Literary Love-Letters, and Other Stories. New York: Scribner, 1897.
The Man Who Wins. New York: Scribner, 1897.
The Gospel of Freedom. New York: Macmillan, 1898.
Love's Dilemmas. Chicago: H. S. Stone, 1898.
The Web of Life. New York: Macmillan, 1900.
The Real World. New York: Macmillan, 1901.
Their Child. New York: Macmillan, 1903.
The Common Lot. New York: Macmillan, 1904.
The Memoirs of an American Citizen. New York: Macmillan, 1905.
The Master of the Inn. New York: Scribner, 1908.
Together. New York: Macmillan, 1908.
A Life for a Life. New York: Macmillan, 1910.
The Healer. New York: Macmillan, 1911.
His Great Adventure. New York: Macmillan, 1913.
One Woman's Life. New York: Macmillan, 1913.
Clark's Field. Boston: Houghton Mifflin, 1914.
The Conscript Mother. New York: Scribner, 1916.
The World Decision. Boston: Houghton Mifflin, 1916.
Homely Lilla. New York: Harcourt, Brace, 1923.
Waste. New York: Harcourt, Brace, 1924.
Wanderings. New York: Harcourt, Brace, 1925.
Chimes. New York: Macmillan, 1926.
Little Black Dog. Chicago: Thos. S. Rockwell, 1931.
The End of Desire. New York: Farrar & Rinehart, 1932.
Sometime. New York: Farrar & Rinehart, 1933.

2. Short Stories

"Literary Love-Letters: Excerpts," *Atlantic Monthly*, LXXIV (December, 1894), 814–25.

"A Question in Art," *Scribner's Magazine*, XVII (April, 1895), 514–24.
"The Price of Romance," *Scribner's Magazine*, XVIII (July, 1895), 60–70.
"The Emigration of the Calkins," syndicated by the Century Association in 1895.
"The Rejected Titian," *Scribner's Magazine*, XXII (July, 1897), 29–36.
"A Pension Love Story," *Scribner's Magazine*, XXII (December, 1897), 740–57.
"A Bull Market," *Saturday Evening Post*, CLXXII (January 27, 1900), 655–57, 678–79.
"Mother Sims," *Saturday Evening Post*, CLXXIII (November 17, 1900), 10–11, 19.
"The Professor's Chance," *Atlantic Monthly*, LXXXVII (May, 1901), 723–32.
"The Polity of Nature," *Lippincott's Magazine*, LXVIII (October, 1901), 458–71.
"Common Honesty," *Saturday Evening Post*, CLXXVI (September 19, 1903), 2–5, 28–30.
"The End of Desire," *Atlantic Monthly*, XCII (October, 1903), 462–69.
"Avalanche," *Scribner's Magazine*, XLI (June, 1907), 705–14.
"Papa's Stratagem," *Collier's*, XL (October 19, 1907), 21–23.
"The Master of the Inn," *Scribner's Magazine*, XLII (December, 1907), 669–81.
"In the Doctor's Office," *Scribner's Magazine*, XLIII (January, 1908), 105–15.
"The General Manager," *Scribner's Magazine*, XLIII (March, 1908), 270–82.
"The Temple of Juno," *Atlantic Monthly*, CI (March, 1908), 353–60.
"Found Out," *Saturday Evening Post*, CLXXXIII (March 25, 1911), 16–17, 57–58.
"The Miracle," *Harper's Monthly*, CXXIV (December, 1911), 138–47.
"His Leetle Trees," *Everybody's Magazine*, XXVII (July, 1912), 35–44.
"The Rainbow Chasers," *Canadian Magazine*, XLIV (December, 1914), 175–86.
"The Conscript Mother," *Scribner's Magazine*, LIX (May, 1916), 574–90.

3. *Literary Essays and Book Reviews*

"Ludovic Halévy," Critical introduction. Ludovic Halévy, *Abbé Constantin and A Marriage for Love*. New York: P. F. Collier, 1902. pp. v–xxi.
"Samuel Richardson," *Dial*, XXXII (April 1, 1902), 243–44.

"The Background of the American Novel," *Yale Review*, N.S., III (January, 1914), 213–33.

"The American Novel," *Yale Review*, N.S., III (April, 1914), 419–37.

"Mrs. Wharton's World," *New Republic*, II (February 13, 1915), 40–42.

"A Late Victorian in Ohio," *New Republic*, II (March 13, 1915), 152–54; a review of Mary S. Watts's *Nathan Burke*.

"Henry Sydnor Harrison," *New Republic*, II (March 27, 1915), 199–201.

"Commercializing the Sex Instinct," in Joyce Kilmer, ed., *Literature in the Making*. New York: Harper, 1917. Pp. 131–41.

"War and American Literature," *Dial*, LXIV (January 3, 1918), 7–8.

"New England and the Novel," *Nation*, CXI (September 18, 1920), 323–25.

"The New Novel," *New Republic*, XXX (April 12, 1922), Literary Supplement, 17–20. Appears also in *The Novel of Tomorrow*. Indianapolis: Bobbs-Merrill, 1922. Pp. 91–102.

"Tolstoi and Henry James," *Yale Review*, N.S., XII (December, 1922), 181–86; a review of Percy Lubbock's *The Craft of Fiction*.

"A Visit to Henry James," *Yale Review*, N.S., XII (July, 1923), 724–41.

"An Author's Models," *Literary Review*, III (August 18, 1923), 905–6.

"Some European Novels in Translation," *Yale Review*, N.S., XIV (January, 1925), 366–73.

Preface to Jack Black. *You Can't Win*. New York: Macmillan, 1926.

"Simplification," *New Republic*, LIII (Jan. 11, 1928), 277; a review of Upton Sinclair's *Money Writes*.

"Why American Literature Is Insignificant," in the English section of the Yiddish *Forward*, March 4, 1928, p. 1.

"The Perfect Lover," *New Republic*, LVI (October 10, 1928), 214; on Murasaki Shikibu's *Tale of Genji*.

"The Drift of the Current," *Bookman*, LXVIII (December, 1928), 377–82.

"A Feline World," *Bookman*, LXIX (March, 1929), 1–6.

"Hermaphrodites," *Bookman*, LXIX (July, 1929), 485–89.

"Fiction and Ideas," *Bookman*, LXIX (July, 1929), 543–48.

"What Is Dirt?" *Bookman*, LXX (November, 1929), 258–62.

"What Is Happening to Our Fiction?" *Nation*, CXXIX (December 4, 1929), 673–74.

"Back Bay Humanist," *New Republic*, LXI (January 1, 1930), 174–75; a review of Edwin Arlington Robinson, ed., *The Letters of Thomas Sergeant Perry*.

Untitled article, *Portland Evening News*, November 8, 1930, p. 5; a review of Mazo De La Roche's *Portrait of a Dog*.

"Dreiseriana," *Saturday Review of Literature*, VII (June 6, 1931), 875; a review of Theodore Dreiser's *Dawn*.

"Civil War Alabama," *Saturday Review of Literature*, VII (April 4, 1931), 708; a review of T. S. Stribling's *The Forge*.

"The Necessity of Anonymity," *Saturday Review of Literature*, VII (June 6, 1931), 886.

"A Sound Tradition," *Saturday Review of Literature*, VIII (September 19, 1931), 131; a review of F. O. Mann's *Albert Grope*.

"The Booze Age," *New Republic*, LXVIII (October 7, 1931), 213–14; a review of Upton Sinclair's *The Wet Parade*.

"The Works of Mrs. Woolf," *Saturday Review of Literature*, VIII (December 5, 1931), 346.

"Henry James," in John Macy, ed., *American Writers on American Literature*. New York: Liveright, 1931. Pp. 298–316.

"Writers in the Jungle," *New Republic*, LXXX (October 17, 1934), 259–61.

"Mark Twain and the American Tradition," *Mark Twain Quarterly*, II (Winter, 1937), 8–11.

4. *Political and Social Essays*

"Mr. Herrick on Armament," *New Republic*, I (December 19, 1914), 22.

"Recantation of a Pacifist," *New Republic*, IV (October 30, 1915), 328–30.

"A Soldier Pacifist," *Scribner's Magazine*, LXII (August, 1917), 247–50.

Introduction. *Poèmes des Poilus*. Boston: Butterfield, 1917.

"Unromantic War," *Dial*, LXIV (February 14, 1918), 133–34.

"The Paper War," *Dial*, LXVI (February 8, 1919), 113–14.

"That Sort of American," *New Republic*, XXII (March 31, 1920), 153–54.

"For Hoover," *Nation*, CX (June 5, 1920), 750–51.

"The Ten Commandments, Again," *New Republic*, XXIII (June 16, 1920), 90–91.

"Telling the Truth About War," *Nation*, CX (June 26, 1920), 850a–51a.

"In General," *Nation*, CXIII (December 7, 1921), 658–59.

"The State of Maine–'Down East'," *Nation*, CXV (August 23, 1922), 182–83.

"The Race Problem in the Caribbean," *Nation*, CXVIII (June 11, 1924), 675–76, and (June 18, 1924), 699–700.

"The War and Ourselves," *Survey*, LII (August 1, 1924), 493–95.

"Advising U.S. to Get Out of Haiti, Prof. Herrick Accuses Marines," New York *World*, April 10, 1927, p. 11E.

"Magic, Black and White," *New Republic*, LVII (January 30, 1929), 298–99.

"Our Super-Babbit: A Recantation," *Nation*, CXXXI (July 16, 1930), 60–62.

"America: The False Messiah," Samuel D. Schmalhausen, ed., *Behold America*! New York: Farrar & Rinehart, 1931. Pp. 53–66.

"Let Us Talk About Unpleasant Things," *Harper's Monthly*, CLXV (October, 1932), 598–604.

"Death of a Puritan," *Nation*, CXXXVI (May 31, 1933), 612–13.

" 'I Don't Believe in Democracy,' " *Nation*, CXXXVII (July 26, 1933), 103–4.

"The American Way," *Partisan Review and Anvil*, III (April, 1936), 7–8.

5. *Academic Writings*

"Effect of the Quarter System on Courses in English Composition," *Educational Review*, VIII (November, 1894), 382–87.

"The University of Chicago," *Scribner's Magazine*, XVIII (October, 1895), 399–417.

Preface to *Silas Marner*, by George Eliot. New York: Longmans, Green, 1895.

Composition and Rhetoric for Schools. Chicago: Scott, Foresman, 1899 (new editions in 1901, 1902, 1911, 1922). With Lindsay Todd Damon.

"Methods of Teaching Rhetoric in Schools," *Teaching English*. Chicago: Scott, Foresman, 1899.

Preface to *Twice-Told Tales*, by Nathaniel Hawthorne. Chicago: Scott, Foresman, 1903. With Robert W. Bruère.

Preface to *The House of Seven Gables*, by Nathaniel Hawthorne. Chicago: Scott, Foresman, 1904.

Manuscripts

The Robert Herrick Papers in the University of Chicago Library are unusually rich in teaching notes, working notebooks, drafts of novels and short stories, aborted projects, unpublished plays, autobiographical sequences, texts for public lectures, personal letters, clippings, and biographical documents. These materials are fully accessible, and no intensive study of Herrick can afford to ignore them. Their richness defies any brief listing.

SECONDARY SOURCES

AARON, DANIEL, ed. *The Memoirs of an American Citizen*. Cambridge: Harvard University Press, 1963. Shrewd, informed introduction to Herrick's best-known novel.

ARVIN, NEWTON. "Homage to Robert Herrick," *New Republic*, LXXXII (March 6, 1935), 93–95. Eloquent, admiring, and perceptive.

BALDWIN, C. C. *The Men Who Make Our Novels*. Rev. ed. New York: Dodd, Mead, 1924. Much autobiographical commentary included with a general assessment.

BERTHOFF, WARNER. *The Ferment of Realism: American Literature, 1884–1919*. New York: Free Press, 1965. Extremely perceptive in spite of the limited space devoted to Herrick.

BJÖRKMAN, EDWIN. "Two Studies of Robert Herrick," *Voices of Tomorrow*. New York: Mitchell Kennerley, 1913. Capable, though critical of Herrick's development.

CARGILL, OSCAR. *Intellectual America: Ideas on the March*. New York: Macmillan, 1941. On the modernism of Herrick's ideas.

COOPER, FREDERICK TABER. "Representative American Story-Tellers: Robert Herrick," *Bookman*, XXVIII (December, 1908), 350–57. Expanded and reprinted in F. T. Cooper, *Some American Story-Tellers*. New York: Holt, 1911. Early commentary.

DELL, FLOYD. "Chicago in Fiction," *Bookman*, XXXVIII (November, 1913), 270–77. Incidental but suggestive on Chicago motif.

DUFFEY, BERNARD. *The Chicago Renaissance in American Letters*. East Lansing: Michigan State College Press, 1954. Excellent on Herrick's relations with "Chicago school."

DUNCAN, HUGH D. *The Rise of Chicago as a Literary Center from 1885 to 1920: A Sociological Essay in American Culture*. Totowa, New Jersey: The Bedminster Press, 1964. Much incidental comment on Herrick, from an extraliterary viewpoint.

GENTHE, CHARLES V. "Robert Herrick (1868–1938)," *American Literary Realism, 1870–1910*, No. 1 (Fall, 1967), 56–61. A selective, annotated bibliography. See also Douglas O. Carlson, "Robert Herrick: An Addendum," *American Literary Realism, 1870–1910* No. 3 (Summer, 1968), 67–68.

HALE, SWINBURNE. "Mr. Robert Herrick and His Realism," *Harvard Monthly*, XXXVI (May, 1903), 105–11. Early praise for Herrick as craftsman.

HARLOW, VIRGINIA. *Thomas Sergeant Perry*. Durham: Duke University Press, 1950. Holds useful background material and also a revealing letter.

HICKS, GRANVILLE. *The Great Tradition*. New York: Macmillan, 1933. Marxist judgment on social attitudes behind the novels.

HOLLAND, ROBERT A. *"Together*: A Nietzschean Novel," *Sewanee Review*, XVI (October, 1908), 495–504. An overwrought attack.

HOWELLS, WILLIAM DEAN. "The Novels of Robert Herrick," *North American Review*, CLXXXIX (June, 1909), 812–20. A milestone in growth of Herrick's contemporary reputation.

JACKSON, KENNY A. "Robert Herrick's Use of Chicago," *Midcontinent American Studies Journal*, V (Spring, 1964), 24–32. Clear and sound, but limited in scope.

KAZIN, ALFRED. *On Native Grounds*. New York: Reynal & Hitchcock. 1942. Persuasive defense, though not unqualified.

KNIGHT, GRANT C. *The Strenuous Age in American Literature*. Chapel Hill: University of North Carolina Press, 1954. Strong but informed praise of Herrick's realism.

KRUTCH, JOSEPH WOOD. "The Long Journey," *Nation*, CXXI (October 7, 1925), 388–89. Review article with wider, admiring perspective.

KUNITZ, STANLEY J., ed. *Authors Today and Yesterday*. New York: H. W. Wilson, 1933. Prints some late autobiographical commentary.

LASCH, CHRISTOPHER. *The New Radicalism in America*. New York: Knopf, 1965. Abrasively suggestive on the rebellion of middle-class intellectuals in Herrick's day.

LOVETT, ROBERT MORSS. *All Our Years*. New York: Viking, 1948. The autobiography of Herrick's closest friend; invaluable for background material.

LÜDEKE, H. "Robert Herrick, Novelist of American Democracy," *English Studies*, XVIII (April, 1936), 49–57. Reprinted in H. Lüdeke, *The "Democracy" of Henry Adams and Other Essays*. Bern: A. Francke, 1950. One of firmest, soundest estimates.

LYNN, KENNETH S. *The Dream of Success*. Boston: Little, Brown, 1955. Detailed, stimulating discussion of one facet; debatable in conclusions.

MAY, HENRY F. *The End of American Innocence*. New York: Knopf, 1959. Excellent cultural and intellectual history for Herrick's most productive years.

NEVIUS, BLAKE. *Robert Herrick: The Development of a Novelist*. Berkeley and Los Angeles: University of California Press, 1962. Definitive biography with much excellent criticism.

NIELSEN, HARALD. "The Novels of Herrick," *Poet-Lore*, XIX (Autumn, 1908), 337–63. Early, extravagant praise by a Danish critic.

NUTLEY, GRACE STUART. "The Social Criticism of Robert Herrick." New York University, doctoral dissertation, 1945. Close, schematic gathering of attitudes on current society.

PATTEE, FRED LEWIS. *The New American Literature 1890–1930*. New York: Century, 1930. Pithy assessment that approached Herrick as a still active rather than embalmed novelist.

PEARCE, RICHARD A. "Chicago in the Fiction of the 1890's as Illustrated in the Novels of Henry B. Fuller and Robert Herrick." Columbia University, doctoral dissertation, 1963. On the very early novels, as regional commentary.

SELDES, GILBERT V. "The American Novel, Part II," *Harvard Monthly*, LVI (March, 1913), 1–11. Perceptive, though mostly unfavorable.

SMITH, HENRY NASH. "The Search for a Capitalist Hero: Businessmen in American Fiction," *The Business Establishment* (Earl F. Cheit, ed.). New York: Wiley, 1964. Fresh analysis of Herrick's advances on fictional treatment of the capitalist.

SPANGLER, GEORGE M. "The Theme of Salvation in the Novels of Robert Herrick." University of California at Berkeley, doctoral dissertation, 1965. Takes up the vital question of Herrick as a "man of piety"; coherent and cogent.

TAYLOR, WALTER FULLER. "The Humanism of Robert Herrick," *American Literature*, XXVIII (November, 1956), 287–301. On central pattern of Herrick's ethics; perhaps overstated but sound.

THOMPSON, RICHARD JOSEPH. "Themes and Tendencies in the Social Criticism of Robert Herrick." State University of New York at Buffalo, doctoral dissertation, 1964. Useful survey that adds up to some insightful and favorable conclusions, especially on Herrick's social foresight and his influence.

TOWERS, TOM H. "Self and Society in the Novels of Robert Herrick," *Journal of Popular Culture*, I (Fall, 1967), 141–57. Capable argument that Herrick increasingly sacrificed social and humane values to the rigors of selfhood.

VAN DOREN, CARL. *The American Novel, 1789–1939*. New York: Macmillan, 1940. Judicious placing of Herrick within the mainstream of American fiction.

WAGENKNECHT, EDWARD. *Cavalcade of the American Novel*. New York: Holt, 1952. Most generous estimate by any historian of American fiction.

YUNCK, JOHN A. "The Natural History of a Dead Quarrel: Hemingway and the Naturalists," *South Atlantic Quarterly*, LXII (Winter, 1963), 28–42. Only tangential to Herrick but illuminating.

Index

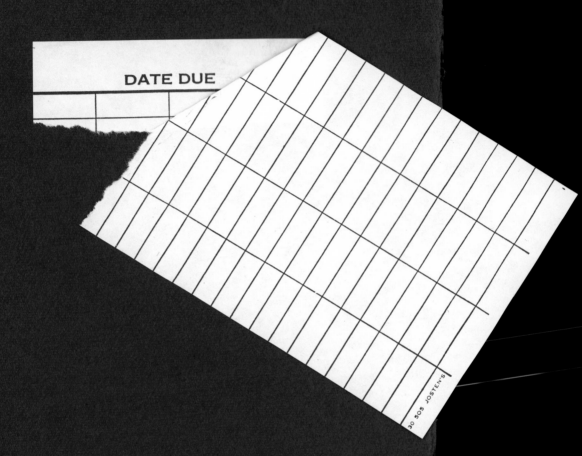

DATE DUE

30 505 JOSTEN'S